Special Education: Core Knowledge Study Guide

► ► ► ► ► ► ► ► ► ► ► ►

A PUBLICATION OF EDUCATIONAL TESTING SERVICE

Table of Contents

Study Guide for the Praxis *Special Education: Core Knowledge* Tests

▶　▶　▶　▶　▶　▶　▶　▶　▶　▶　▶　▶

TABLE OF CONTENTS

Chapter 1

Introduction to the *Special Education: Core Knowledge* Tests and Suggestions for Using this Study Guide 1

Chapter 2

Background Information on The Praxis Series™ Assessments 7

Chapter 3

Study Topics for the *Special Education: Core Knowledge* Tests 13

Chapter 4

Don't Be Defeated by Multiple-Choice Questions 31

Chapter 5

Practice Questions for the *Special Education: Core Knowledge* Tests 41

Chapter 6

Right Answers and Explanations for the *Special Education: Core Knowledge* Practice Questions 59

Chapter 7

Are You Ready? Last-Minute Tips 75

Appendix A

Study Plan Sheet 79

Appendix B

For More Information 83

Chapter 1

Introduction to the *Special Education: Core Knowledge* Tests and Suggestions for Using this Study Guide

▶ ▶ ▶ ▶ ▶ ▶ ▶ ▶ ▶ ▶ ▶ ▶

Special Education 0350, 0352, 0351, 0353

Introduction to the *Special Education: Core Knowledge* Tests

The *Special Education: Core Knowledge* tests are designed for prospective secondary special education teachers. The tests are designed to reflect current standards for knowledge, skills, and abilities in special education. Educational Testing Service (ETS) works in collaboration with the Council for Exceptional Children (CEC), along with teacher educators, higher education content specialists, and accomplished practicing teachers in the field of special education to keep the tests updated and representative of current standards.

There are four different *Special Education: Core Knowledge* tests covered in this guide:

- *Special Education* (0350)
- *Special Education: Application of Core Principles Across Categories of Disability* (0352)
- *Special Education: Knowledge-Based Core Principles* (0351)
- *Special Education Core Principles: Content Knowledge* (0353)

The *Special Education* test (0350) consists of 150 multiple-choice questions and covers five major areas, in the following proportions:

- Understanding Exceptionalities (10%)
- Legal Aspects of Special Education (10%)
- Assessment and Evaluation in Special Education (20%)
- Service Delivery and Instruction (37%)
- Classroom Management and Student Behavior (23%)

Test takers have two hours to complete the test.

The *Special Education: Application of Core Principles Across Categories of Disability* test (0352) consists of 50 multiple-choice questions and covers five major areas, in the following proportions:

- Curriculum (20%)
- Instruction (20%)
- Assessment (20%)
- Managing the Learning Environment (20%)
- Professional Roles/Issues/Literature (20%)

Test takers have one hour to complete the test.

The *Special Education: Knowledge-Based Core Principles* test (0351) consists of 60 multiple-choice questions and covers three major areas, in the following proportions:

- Understanding Exceptionalities (25%)
- Legal and Societal Issues (13%)
- Delivery of Services to Students with Disabilities (62%)

Test takers have one hour to complete the test.

The *Special Education Core Principles: Content Knowledge* test (0353) consists of 60 multiple-choice questions and covers three major areas, in the following proportions:

- Understanding Exceptionalities (25-30%)
- Legal and Societal Issues (15-20%)
- Delivery of Services to Students with Disabilities (50-60%)

Test takers have one hour to complete the test.

None of the tests is intended to assess teaching skills but rather to demonstrate the candidate's fundamental knowledge in the major areas of special education.

Suggestions for Using the "Study Topics" Chapter of this Study Guide

The *Special Education: Core Knowledge* test you will take is different from a final exam or other tests you may have taken in that it is comprehensive — that is, it covers material you may have learned in several courses during more than one year. It requires you to synthesize information you have learned from many sources and to understand the subject as a whole.

This test is also very different from the SAT® or other assessments of your reading, writing, and mathematical skills. You may have heard it said that you can't study for the SAT — that is, you should have learned these skills throughout your school years, and you can't learn reading or reasoning skills shortly before you take the exam. You can *practice* taking the SAT and skills tests like it to become more adept at applying the skills to the particular format of the test. The *Special Education: Core Knowledge* tests, on the other hand, assess a domain you can review for and can prepare to be tested on. Therefore, you should review for and prepare for your test, not merely practice with the question formats. A thorough review of the material covered on the test will significantly increase your likelihood of success. Moreover, studying for your licensing exam is a great opportunity to reflect on your field and develop a deeper understanding of it before you begin to teach the subject matter to others. As you prepare to take the test, you may find it particularly helpful to think about how you would apply the study topics and sample exercises to your own clinical experience that you obtained in schools during your teacher preparation program. Your student teaching experience will be especially relevant to your thinking about the materials in the study guide.

We recommend the following approach for using the "Study Topics" chapters to prepare for the test.

Become familiar with the test content. Learn what will be assessed in the test, covered in chapter 3.

Assess how well you know the content in each subject area. It is quite likely that you will need to study in most or all of the areas. After you learn what the test contains, you should assess your knowledge in each area. How well do you know the material? In which areas do you need to learn more before you take the test?

Develop a study plan. Assess what you need to study and create a realistic plan for studying. You can develop your study plan in any way that works best for you. A "Study Plan" form is included in Appendix A at the end of the book as a possible way to structure your planning. Remember that this is a licensure test and covers a great deal of material. Plan to review carefully. You will need to allow time to find the books and other materials, time to read the material and take notes, and time to go over your notes.

Identify study materials. Most of the material covered by the test is contained in standard introductory textbooks. If you do not own introductory texts that cover all the areas, you may want to borrow one or more from friends or from a library. You may also want to obtain a copy of your state's standards for special education. (One way to find these standards quickly is to go to the Web site for your state's Department of Education.) The textbooks used in secondary classrooms may also prove useful to you, since they also present the material you need to know. Use standard school and college introductory textbooks and other reliable, professionally prepared materials. Don't rely heavily on information provided by friends or from searching the World Wide Web. Neither of these sources is as uniformly reliable as textbooks.

Work through your study plan. You may want to work alone, or you may find it more helpful to work with a group or with a mentor. Work through the topics and questions provided in chapter 3. Be able to define and discuss the topics in your own words rather than memorizing definitions from books. If you are working with a group or mentor, you can also try informal quizzes and questioning techniques.

Proceed to the practice questions. Once you have completed your review, you are ready to benefit from the "Practice Questions" portion of this guide.

Suggestions for using the "Practice Questions" and "Right Answers and Explanations for the Practice Questions" Chapters

Read chapter 4 ("Don't Be Defeated by Multiple-Choice Questions"). This chapter will sharpen your skills in reading and answering questions. Succeeding on multiple-choice questions requires careful focus on the question, an eye for detail, and patient sifting of the answer choices.

Answer the practice questions in chapter 5. Make your own test-taking conditions as similar to actual testing conditions as you can. Work on the practice questions in a quiet place without distractions. Remember that the practice questions are only examples of the way the topics are covered in the test. The test you take will have different questions.

Score the practice questions. Go through the detailed answers in chapter 6 ("Right Answers and Explanations") and mark the questions you answered correctly and the ones you missed. Look over the explanations of the questions you missed and see whether you understand them.

Decide whether you need more review. After you have looked at your results, decide whether you need to brush up on certain subject areas before taking the actual test. Go back to your textbooks and reference materials to see whether the topics are covered there. You might also want to go over your questions with a friend or teacher who is familiar with the subjects.

Assess your readiness. Do you feel confident about your level of understanding in each of the areas? If not, where do you need more work? If you feel ready, complete the checklist in chapter 7 ("Are You Ready?") to double-check that you've thought through the details. If you need more information about registration or the testing situation itself, use the resources in Appendix B: "For More Information."

Chapter 2
Background Information on
The Praxis Series™ Assessments

▶   ▶   ▶   ▶   ▶   ▶   ▶   ▶   ▶   ▶   ▶   ▶

What are The Praxis Series Subject Assessments?

The Praxis Series Subject Assessments are designed by Educational Testing Service (ETS) to assess your knowledge of the subject area you plan to teach, and they are a part of the licensing procedure in many states. This study guide covers an assessment that tests your knowledge of the actual content you hope to be licensed to teach. Your state has adopted The Praxis Series tests because it wants to be certain that you have achieved a specified level of mastery of your subject area before it grants you a license to teach in a classroom.

The Praxis Series tests are part of a national testing program, meaning that the test covered in this study guide is used in more than one state. The advantage of taking Praxis tests is that if you want to move to another state that uses The Praxis Series tests, you can transfer your scores to that state. Passing scores are set by states, however, so if you are planning to apply for licensure in another state, you may find that passing scores are different. You can find passing scores for all states that use The Praxis Series tests in the *Understanding Your Praxis Scores* pamphlet, available either in your college's School of Education or by calling (609) 771-7395.

What is licensure?

Licensure in any area — medicine, law, architecture, accounting, cosmetology — is an assurance to the public that the person holding the license has demonstrated a certain level of competence. The phrase used in licensure is that the person holding the license *will do no harm*. In the case of teacher licensing, a license tells the public that the person holding the license can be trusted to educate children competently and professionally.

Because a license makes such a serious claim about its holder, licensure tests are usually quite demanding. In some fields licensure tests have more than one part and last for more than one day. Candidates for licensure in all fields plan intensive study as part of their professional preparation: some join study groups, others study alone. But preparing to take a licensure test is, in all cases, a professional activity. Because it assesses your entire body of knowledge or skill for the field you want to enter, preparing for a licensure exam takes planning, discipline, and sustained effort. Studying thoroughly is highly recommended.

Why does my state require The Praxis Series Assessments?

Your state chose The Praxis Series Assessments because the tests assess the breadth and depth of content — called the "domain" of the test — that your state wants its teachers to possess before they begin to teach. The level of content knowledge, reflected in the passing score, is based on recommendations of panels of teachers and teacher educators in each subject area in each state. The state licensing agency and, in some states, the state legislature ratify the passing scores that have been recommended by panels of teachers.

You can find out the passing score required for The Praxis Series Assessments in your state by looking in the pamphlet *Understanding Your Praxis Scores*, which is free from ETS (see above). If you look through this pamphlet, you will see that not all states use the same test modules, and even when they do, the passing scores can differ from state to state.

What kinds of tests are The Praxis Series Subject Assessments?

Two kinds of tests comprise The Praxis Series Subject Assessments: multiple choice (for which you select your answer from a list of choices) and constructed response (for which you write a response of your own). Multiple-choice tests can survey a wider domain because they can ask more questions in a limited period of time. Constructed-response tests have far fewer questions, but the questions require you to demonstrate the depth of your knowledge in the area covered.

What do the tests measure?

The Praxis Series Subject Assessments are tests of content knowledge. They measure your understanding of the subject area you want to teach. The multiple-choice tests measure a broad range of knowledge across your content area. The constructed-response tests measure your ability to explain in depth a few essential topics in your subject area. The content-specific pedagogy tests, most of which are constructed-response, measure your understanding of how to teach certain fundamental concepts in your field. The tests do not measure your actual teaching ability, however. They measure your knowledge of your subject and of how to teach it. The teachers in your field who help us design and write these tests, and the states that require these tests, do so in the belief that knowledge of subject area is the first requirement for licensing. Your teaching ability is a skill that is measured in other ways: observation, videotaped teaching, or portfolios are typically used by states to measure teaching ability. Teaching combines many complex skills, only some of which can be measured by a single test. The Praxis Series Subject Assessments are designed to measure how thoroughly you understand the material in the subject areas in which you want to be licensed to teach.

How were these tests developed?

ETS began the development of The Praxis Series Subject Assessments with a survey. For each subject, teachers around the country in various teaching situations were asked to judge which knowledge and skills a beginning teacher in that subject needs to possess. Professors in schools of education who prepare teachers were asked the same questions. These responses were ranked in order of importance and sent out to hundreds of teachers for review. All of the responses to these surveys (called "job analysis surveys") were analyzed to summarize the judgments of these professionals. From their consensus, we developed the specifications for the multiple-choice and constructed-response tests. Each subject area had a committee of practicing teachers and teacher educators who wrote these specifications (guidelines). The specifications were reviewed and eventually approved by teachers. From the test specifications, groups of teachers and professional test developers created test questions.

When your state adopted The Praxis Series Subject Assessments, local panels of practicing teachers and teacher educators in each subject area met to examine the tests question by question and evaluate each question for its relevance to beginning teachers in your state. This is called a "validity study." A test is considered "valid" for a job if it measures what people must know and be able to do on that job. For the test to be adopted in your state, teachers in your state must judge that it is valid.

These teachers and teacher educators also performed a "standard-setting study"; that is, they went through the tests question by question and decided, through a rigorous process, how many questions a beginning teacher would be able to answer correctly. From this study emerged a recommended passing score. The final passing score was approved by your state's licensing agency.

In other words, throughout the development process, practitioners in the teaching field — teachers and teacher educators — have determined what the tests would contain. The practitioners in your state determined which tests would be used for licensure in your subject area and helped decide what score would be needed to achieve licensure. This is how professional licensure works in most fields: those who are already licensed oversee the licensing of new practitioners. When you pass The Praxis Series Subject Assessments, you and the practitioners in your state can be assured that you have the knowledge required to begin practicing your profession.

Chapter 3
Study Topics for the *Special Education:*
Core Knowledge Tests

► ► ► ► ► ► ► ► ► ► ►

Introduction to the test

The *Special Education: Core Knowledge* tests are designed to measure the subject-area knowledge and competencies necessary for a beginning teacher of special education in a K-12 setting. The topics for questions are typically those covered in introductory college-level special education courses, although some questions of a more advanced nature are included. The questions include definition of terms, comprehension of critical concepts, application, analysis, and problem solving. All the questions on the test are multiple-choice and require you to select an answer from a set of four or five options.

This chapter is intended to help you organize your preparation for the test and to give you a clear indication about the depth and breadth of the knowledge required for success on the tests.

Using the topic lists that follow: You are not expected to be an expert on all aspects of the topics that follow. You should understand the major characteristics of each topic, recognize the minor topics, and have some familiarity with the subtopics. Virtually all accredited undergraduate or graduate special education programs address the majority of these topics, subtopics, and even minor topics. Moreover, the content of *Special Education Core Principles: Content Knowledge* generally parallels the Common Core Knowledge and Skills Statements of the Council for Exceptional Children's (CEC) Special Education Program Standards.

You are relatively likely to find that the organization of your introduction to special education textbook is similar to the organization of the first two topic sections, **Understanding Exceptionalities** and **Legal and Societal Issues.**

For example, under the subtopic, **Basic concepts in special education,** look at

- Definitions of all major categories and specific disabilities, as well as the incidence and prevalence of various types of disabilities
- The causation and prevention of disability
- The nature of behaviors, including frequency, duration, intensity, and degrees of severity
- The classification of students with disabilities

Most introductory texts devote individual chapters to disability categories. Chapters usually begin with definitions, incidence, and prevalence, with some discussion of causation (etiology) and prevention. A description of characteristics, or the nature of the behaviors, generally follows.

Your introductory special education course material provides only a general guide. Consult materials and resources from all your core special education coursework. You should be able to match up specific topics and subtopics with what you have covered in your courses in special education assessment, instructional methods, classroom management, and so on. You will find that the **Delivery of Services to Students with Disabilities** section tends to be organized around main topic areas that are often associated with specific courses. Reviewing minor topics by using the index of a textbook tends to be an effective way to refresh your understanding.

Try not to be overwhelmed by the volume and scope of content knowledge in this guide. An overview such as this that lists special education topics does not offer you a great deal of context. Although a specific term may not seem familiar as you see it here, you might find you could understand it when applied to a real-life situation.

Many of the questions on the actual Praxis test will provide you with a context to apply to these topics or terms. Finally, teaching students with exceptionalities requires common sense. Answers that are technically accurate also tend to be the most logical. As a special education teacher, you should have developed good decision-making skills in addition to your knowledge of content. Apply those skills on the test. You may know more than you think.

Special questions marked with stars:
Interspersed throughout the list of topics are questions that are outlined in boxes and preceded by stars (★). These questions are intended to help you test your knowledge of fundamental concepts and your ability to apply fundamental concepts to typical classroom situations. Most of the questions require you to combine several pieces of knowledge in order to formulate an integrated understanding and response. If you spend time on these questions, you will gain increased understanding and facility with the subject matter covered on the test. You might want to discuss these questions and your answers with a teacher or mentor.

Note that the questions marked with stars are not short-answer or multiple-choice. The questions marked with stars are intended as *study* questions, not practice questions. Thinking about the answers to them should improve your understanding of fundamental concepts and will probably help you

answer a broad range of questions on the test. For example, the following box with a star appears in the list of study topics under "classifications as represented in Individuals with Disabilities Education Act [IDEA '97]":

★ What are the 12 categories of disabilities under IDEA '97?

If you think about what IDEA '97 covers and are able to jot down a list of the disability categories included, you have probably prepared yourself to answer multiple-choice questions similar to the one below:

All of the following are components of IDEA '97 EXCEPT:

(A) Physical therapy is available to students with spina bifida.
(B) Mental retardation is subdivided according to an I.Q. score on a standardized test.
(C) The existence of multiple disabilities does not limit the types of services possible for any student.
(D) Children classified as ADD/ADHD must have a behavior management plan as a part of their IEP.

(The correct answer is (D). Under IDEA '97, ADD/ADHD is not a specific disability category, and a behavior management plan may not be necessary for every child.)

Understanding Exceptionalities

An understanding of exceptionalities begins with an understanding of human development. We conceptualize exceptionalities by using normal development as a reference point. Human development encompasses many areas — social and emotional, language, cognition, and physical and sensory. Significant differences or deficits in these areas of development may be indications of exceptionality.

Human development and behavior as related to students with disabilities

- ◆ Social and emotional development and behavior
  - Identifying normal behavior
- ◆ Language development and behavior
  - Early childhood language development
- ◆ Cognition
  - Thinking, knowing, or processing information
  - History of intelligence testing
- ◆ Physical development, including motor and sensory
  - Bodily impairments
  - Differences in vision and hearing that affect performance

★ What does the term *developmental disabilities* mean?

★ What are differences between a developmental delay and a developmental deficit or disorder?

Many textbooks define the exceptional child as one who is different from a normal child in terms of mental (or cognitive) characteristics, sensory abilities, communication abilities, behavioral and emotional development, or physical characteristics (Kirk, Gallagher, & Anastasiow, 2000). Cultural and socioeconomic factors often interact with these characteristics, raising additional educational considerations. Exceptional children remind us of the many ways children develop and learn. Teaching exceptional children expands our ability to teach all children.

Characteristics of students with disabilities, including the influence of

- ◆ Cognitive factors
- ◆ Affective and social-adaptive factors, including cultural, linguistic, gender, and socioeconomic factors
- ◆ Genetic, medical, motor, sensory, and chronological-age factors

★ How is it that individuals with the same disability can differ in the way they learn?

★ What is the impact of chronological-age factors?

In most cases, a disability affects many characteristics, cutting across different areas of functioning. Factors that contribute to a disability are also multifaceted. In almost all cases, the characteristics of a disability are the result of some combination of nature and nurture, unique in every individual circumstance. Definitions of a number of different disabilities explicitly reference a range of factors and characteristics.

At a programmatic level, the Individuals with Disabilities Education Act (PL 105-17), known as IDEA '97, defines basic concepts in special education. IDEA '97 defines twelve categories of disability and outlines the fundamental processes of providing services to students who meet these categorical requirements. Many educators have criticized the categorical approach for being exclusionary and have questioned its educational relevance.

Basic concepts in special education, including

- ▶ Definitions of all major categories and specific disabilities, as well as the incidence and prevalence of various types of disabilities
  - Mental retardation
  - Specific learning disabilities
  - Serious emotional disturbances
  - Speech or language impairments
  - Vision impairments
  - Hearing impairments
  - Orthopedic impairments
  - Other health impairments
  - Deafness-blindness
  - Multiple disabilities
  - Autism
  - Traumatic brain injury

> ★ Be able to identify the basic characteristics or defining factors for each type of disability.
>
> ★ Is there only one definition for each category of specific disability?

- ▶ Understanding people with disabilities
  - Medical model
  - Psychological model
  - Sociological model
- ▶ The causation and prevention of disability
  - Biological perspectives
  - Behavioral perspectives
  - Psychodynamic perspectives
  - Sociological-ecological approach
- ▶ Dimensions by which behaviors are measured
  - Frequency
  - Duration
  - Intensity
  - Degrees of severity

> ★ What are some basic assumptions underlying behavioral approaches?

- ▶ The classification of students with disabilities
  - Classifications as represented in Individuals with Disabilities Education Act (IDEA '97)

> ★ What are the twelve categories of disabilities under IDEA '97?

  - Labeling of students

> ★ Labeling students with disabilities has been controversial since the passage of PL 94-142. What are some major arguments for and against labeling?

— Developmental approach

— Cultural approach

— Individual approach

- ADHD

★ What does IDEA say about ADHD? How do students with ADHD receive educational services?

- The implications of the classification process for the persons classified

★ What is the noncategorical perspective?

◆ The influence of level of severity and presence of multiple exceptionalities on students with disabilities

- Mild, moderate, severe/profound categories within a specific disability

★ No category of disability is a "one size fits all" situation. Degree of severity within a category may be more telling than the category itself. Educational goals, approaches, and considerations for students with severe and multiple disabilities are different from those for students with mild and moderate disabilities. What other possible functions need to be considered in designing education?

The influence of a disabling or exceptional condition does not end after an individual has exited the school system. Disabilities are lifelong conditions, although the effects change with the varied challenges of adulthood. For example, a difficulty with reading in adulthood will not result in labeling, placement, and instruction issues, but it may have a profound impact on the individual's ability to meet the demands of the workplace. Further, the post-school world does not offer the types of supports found in IDEA '97. Adults with disabilities must take a proactive role in understanding their rights under the ADA and in seeking supports and resources they may need. They also must make decisions about the extent to which they identify or consider themselves as "disabled."

The influence of (an) exceptional condition(s) throughout an individual's life span

◆ Theories of life span and adult development

★ Does development end in adulthood?

◆ Education

★ How do we prepare students for adulthood?

- Postsecondary education

- Continuing adult education

◆ Employment

- Unemployment and underemployment

★ What is underemployment, and why is it often a more salient issue than unemployment for many persons with disabilities?

★ What agencies can aid in preparing a student for work?

- Americans with Disabilities Act (ADA)
  — Accessibility and reasonable accommodations
  — Nondiscrimination

◆ Social-Emotional

  • Disclosure of a disability

  • Self-advocacy

◆ Family

  • Continuing dependency

  • Changes in family roles

  • Marriage and parenting

◆ Recreation

Legal and Societal Issues

In many ways, the history of legislation defines the history of services to students with disabilities. Moreover, legislation tends to reflect changing attitudes about and perceptions of persons with disabilities. The philosophy of what constitutes a free and appropriate public education has changed and evolved in the various reauthorizations of the original PL 94-142. Other federal laws address basic issues of civil and individual rights of persons with disabilities. Persons with disabilities have shared in the same struggle for civil rights with other minority and disenfranchised groups.

Federal laws and legal issues related to special education

◆ Public Law 94-142

  • Zero reject (F.A.P.E.)

  • Nondiscriminatory assessment

  • Individualized education

  • Least restrictive environment

  • Due process

  • Parental participation

◆ Public Law 101-476 (IDEA)

★ Why did Congress change the name of the Education of the Handicapped Act to IDEA?

  • Emphasis on inclusion

  • Transition and Individual Transition Plan (ITP)

  • Autism and traumatic brain injury

◆ Public Law 105-17 (IDEA '97)

  • Suspension and expulsion

  • Triennial evaluations not mandated

◆ Section 504

  • Rehabilitation Act of 1973

◆ Americans with Disabilities Act (ADA)

  • Nondiscriminatory employment

  • Public accommodations and access

  • Transportation

  • Telecommunications

  • Government

★ What are differences between Section 504 and the ADA?

★ How do Section 504 and the ADA define disability?

◆ Important legal issues, such as those raised by the following cases:

  • *Rowley* re: program appropriateness

  • *Tatro* re: related services

  • *Honig* re: discipline

  • *Oberti* re: inclusion

Schools are increasingly aware that the purpose of working with children through the first 18 years of their lives is to prepare them for the next 70 years. In order to prepare students to live and work in local communities, schools need to partner with members of those communities — families, employers, and support agencies, networks, and organizations. IDEA '97 requires special educators to take the lead in initiating and coordinating transition planning for students with disabilities, a process that involves considerable interaction with local communities.

The school's connections with the families, prospective and actual employers, and communities of students with disabilities, for example

➧ Teacher advocacy for students and families, developing student self-advocacy

★ What is learned helplessness?

➧ Parent partnerships and roles

• Rights and responsibilities

• Transition planning

• Advocacy organizations, e.g., CEC, LDA, ARC

➧ Public attitudes toward individuals with disabilities

➧ Cultural and community influences on public attitudes toward individuals with disabilities

➧ Interagency agreements

★ What agencies are often involved in transition planning?

➧ Cooperative nature of the transition planning process

★ Who participates in the transition planning process?

The history of special education has a surprising cast of characters. Geraldo Rivera's shattering expose of the Willowbrook School in 1972 was arguably the most powerful single factor in building public support for deinstitutionalization and community-based placements. Over the past 40 to 50 years, a philosophy of inclusion in all areas of life has gradually evolved, represented by changes in legislation as well as public attitudes. In many cases, ongoing advances in technology make inclusion a practical reality. Special educators should be aware of the larger social, political, economic, and educational forces that continue to shape current practices.

Historical movements/trends affecting the connections between special education and the larger society, for example

➧ Deinstitutionalization and community-based placements

★ What does the term *normalization* mean?

➧ Inclusion

★ What are differences between mainstreaming and inclusion?

➧ Application of technology

➧ Transition

• Developmental services

• Vocational rehabilitation

• Sheltered workshops/supported employment

★ What does IDEA '97 mandate regarding transition planning?

- Advocacy
- Accountability and meeting educational standards

Delivery of Services to Students with Disabilities

The approaches a teacher uses to interact with students are directly related to the teacher's theoretical or conceptual orientation. For example, in working to change a student's behavior, a teacher with a behavioral orientation would focus on measuring the behavior and implementing a reward system for improvement. A teacher from a psychodynamic background would spend more time talking with the student, trying to discover the feelings and motivations causing the behavior. In practice, most teachers employ combinations of conceptual approaches. Special education teachers also need to be aware of general issues and trends within the field that drive placement and program issues. Special education teachers are part of a large system. Understanding how and why that system works is an important component of effective teaching.

Background knowledge, including

- Conceptual approaches underlying service delivery to students with disabilities, including
  - Cognitive
  - Constructivist
  - Psychodynamic
  - Behavioral
  - Sociological

- Ecological
- Therapeutic (speech/language, physical, and occupational) and medical approaches

---

★ What combination of approaches do special education teachers typically use?

★ To what extent do these conceptual approaches overlap?

- Placement and program issues such as
  - Early intervention
    — Infants and Toddlers Act (PL 99-457, Part C)
    — Prevention of secondary disabilities
  - Least restrictive environment
  - Inclusion

★ What are the characteristics of schools with successful inclusion programs?

★ What skills do students need for successful inclusion?

- Role of individualized education program (IEP) team

★ Who participates on the IEP team?

- Due process guidelines
- Categorical, noncategorical, and cross-categorical programs

---

★ Distinguish between categorical, noncategorical, and cross-categorical grouping of students.

- Continuum of educational and related services

- Related services and their integration into the classroom, including roles of other professionals

- Accommodations, including access to assistive technology

★ Is assistive technology always "hi-tech"?

- Transition of students into and within special education placements

- Community-based training

- Post-school transitions

◗ Integrating best practices from multidisciplinary research and professional literature into the educational setting

- Cooperative learning

★ Think of a student for whom cooperative learning might not be a good approach. Why not?

- Learning strategies

★ Give an example of a learning strategy.

Developing and implementing curriculum and instruction are the heart of the teaching process. In addition to understanding general teaching models and strategies, a special education teacher should be able to modify and individualize curriculum and instruction to meet the special needs of students with exceptionalities. Special education teachers must be aware of the many dimensions of curriculum and instruction, taking into account instructional formats, type of curriculum, technology, and other factors within the context of the individual needs of the student.

Curriculum and instruction and their implementation across the continuum of educational placements, including

◗ The individualized family service plan (IFSP)/individualized education program (IEP) process

★ What are the differences between the IFSP and the IEP?

◗ Instructional development and implementation, for example

- Instructional activities

- Curricular materials and resources

- Working with classroom and support personnel

★ What is the relationship between a special education teacher and an instructional assistant or paraeducator?

★ What is the relationship between a special education teacher and a general education teacher?

- Tutoring options

◗ Teaching strategies and methods, for example

- Modification of materials and equipment

- Learning centers

- Facilitated groups

- Study skills groups

- Self-management

- Cooperative learning

★ What are the differences between peer/cross-age tutoring and cooperative learning?

- Diagnostic-prescriptive method

★ What are modality or learning style approaches?

★ Why are they controversial?

- Modeling, skill drill
- Guided practice
- Concept generalization
- Learning strategy instruction

★ What is meant by metacognitive approaches, often a component of learning strategy instruction and concept generalization?

- Direct instruction
  — Precisely sequenced lessons
  — Modeling, drill, practice and immediate feedback
  — Teacher-centered
- ▶ Instructional format and components, for example:
  - Small- and large-group instruction
    — Facilitated group strategies
  - Functional academics
  - General academics with focus on special education

★ In many schools, there is no special education curriculum for the majority of students with exceptionalities. Rather, special educators are expected to adapt the general education curriculum to make it accessible for students in special education.

- ESL and limited English proficiency

★ When is special education appropriate for children who speak a language other than English? When is it not appropriate?

- Language and literacy acquisition
- Self-care and daily living skills
- Pre-vocational and vocational skills
- ▶ Career development and transition issues as related to curriculum design and implementation for students with disabilities according to the criteria of ultimate functioning
- Functional academics
- Community-based instruction

★ Community-based instruction is an essential component for the transition from school to the "real world" for many exceptional students. Students often find it easier to learn skills in the settings to which they apply rather than in the classroom. How do teachers arrange for community-based instruction?

- Individual Transition Plan (ITP)

★ Who participates in the development of the ITP?

- ▶ Technology for teaching and learning in special education settings, for example:
  - Integrating assistive technology into the classroom

★ Did you know that assistive technology is not just hi-tech, computer-based adaptations? Can you name lower-tech devices that help students with disabilities adapt to the educational setting?

- Computer-assisted instruction

★Does computer-assisted instruction mean less teacher involvement?

- Augmentative and alternative communication
  — Sign language and gestures (unaided)
  — Communication boards (aided)
- Adaptive access for microcomputers
- Positioning and power mobility for students with physical disabilities
- Accessing and using information technology
- Use of productivity tools
- Technology for sensory disabilities
  — Closed captioning
  — Telecommunication devices
  — Cochlear implant

★ Many deaf persons adamantly oppose the cochlear implant. Do you know why?

  — Closed-circuit television (CCTV)
  — Mobility devices
  — Braille 'n Speak, Optacon Scanner
- Voice-activated, speech-synthesis, speech-recognition, and word-prediction software

★ What are the uses of an assistive technology device such as the Kurzweil Reading Machine?

Special educators interact with assessment in virtually everything they do. Special education begins with assessment, initiated by a referral. All the components of the diagnostic and placement process that follow — observation, screening, formal and informal testing — are types of assessment. The special education teacher needs

to know how to interpret these types of assessments, particularly to gain a sense of the student's strengths, weaknesses, and needs. Once the student enters class, assessment for instructional purposes begins. Teachers generally find that observing and measuring the student's ability on the class curriculum provides relevant information for instructional decision-making. Consequently, teachers need to know how to design or select, implement, and interpret informal assessments. Finally, teachers need to be able to use assessment measures to evaluate the instructional process and determine whether objectives and goals have been met.

Assessment, including

◆ Use of assessment for screening, diagnosis, placement, and making instructional decisions

- How to select and conduct nondiscriminatory and appropriate assessments

★ What are the provisions for nondiscriminatory testing procedures in IDEA '97?

- How to interpret standardized and specialized assessment results
- Understanding of concepts such as
  — Reliability
  — Validity
  — Standard deviation
  — Standard error of measurement
- How to effectively use evaluation results in IFSP/IEP development
- How to prepare written reports and communicate findings

▶ Procedures and test materials, both formal and informal, typically used for pre-referral, screening, referral, classification, placement, and ongoing program monitoring

— Self-evaluation questionnaires and interviews
— Journals and learning logs
— Portfolio assessment

★ How does due process affect pre-referral, screening, referral, classification, placement, and ongoing program monitoring?

▶ How to select, construct, conduct, and modify nondiscriminatory, developmentally and chronologically age-appropriate informal assessments

★ How do teachers use assessment measures as a means for developing appropriate, individualized instruction? What types of tests do they use? How are they constructed?

• Teacher-made tests

★ Why do teachers construct their own tests? How do teachers create reliable and valid tests?

• Criterion-referenced tests

• Curriculum-based assessment

• Informal reading inventories

• Other alternatives to norm-referenced testing

★ What is authentic assessment?

— Observations

★ What are different ways of recording observations?

— Anecdotal records
— Error analysis
— Miscue analysis

★ What might be included in a portfolio assessment of a student? What skills can be assessed using portfolios?

★ When you apply for a teaching position, you may be asked to provide your own portfolio. What are examples of things you would include as a beginning professional? What types of portfolios could you use as a teacher?

Structuring and managing the learning environment are not ends in themselves but means of facilitating efficient and effective instruction. Structuring the learning environment effectively is preventative and proactive teaching at its best. A well-structured environment addresses the arrangement of students, materials, and special areas. For every problem a well-structured class prevents, the teacher is able to devote more time to instruction. Creating a positive environment starts with understanding the individual needs of your students. Obviously, no matter how well the learning environment is structured, special education teachers must have a repertoire of classroom management skills. Most teachers employ some type of behavioral approach. In order to manage or change student behaviors, the teacher must operationalize behaviors so that they are observable and measurable. The teacher then must have a means of recording observations to determine the effectiveness of interventions. Finally, having a range of strategies encompassing behavioral and other (e.g., psychodynamic) perspectives is a critical component of effective classroom management.

Structuring and managing the learning environment, including

❯ Structuring the learning environment

★ What factors should be considered in structuring the learning environment?

★ Consider certain specific cases of students with disabilities. For each one, how would you structure the environment to meet the student's learning needs?

- The physical-social environment for learning
  — Expectations
  — Rules
  — Consequences
  — Consistency
  — Attitudes
  — Lighting
  — Acoustic characteristics
  — Seating
  — Access
  — Safety provisions
  — Strategies for positive interactions

★ How would you arrange a classroom where you and your students can access materials easily, see and hear each other, and engage in active teaching and learning?

- Transitions between lessons and activities

★ What strategies are effective for having students move around the classroom without being disruptive?

- Grouping of students
  — Heterogeneous vs. homogenous grouping

- Integration of related services
  — Occupational therapy
  — Physical therapy
  — Speech and language therapy

★ What are differences between speech and language?

★ According to the U.S. Department of Education, 19 percent of all students receiving services through IDEA have speech or language difficulties, the second most frequently occurring disability next to learning disabilities.

❯ Classroom management techniques

- Behavioral analysis

★ What is the S_1-R-S_2 or the ABC model?
  — Identification and definition of antecedents
  — Target behavior

★ How do you make a behavior measurable?
  — Consequent events
    – Positive reinforcement
    – Negative reinforcement
    – Ignoring
    – Punishment

- Behavioral interventions

★ What are some of the issues surrounding the use of punishment?

- Functional analysis

★ How does identifying the antecedent, the consequence, and the conditions under which the behavior occurs help a teacher develop an intervention?

- Data-gathering procedures
  — Anecdotal data
  — Frequency methods
  — Interval methods
  — Duration methods

- Self-management strategies and reinforcement

- Cognitive-behavioral interventions

- Psychoeducational models
  — Life space interview

- Social skills training

★ How important is social skills training? Research indicates that successful adaptation to adulthood relies more on effective social and interpersonal skills than on academic or even vocational skills. As many students with exceptionalities have deficits in social skills, facilitating social skills development is a paramount teaching responsibility in preparing students for the world beyond school. Special education teachers need to be familiar with a variety of instructional approaches in this area.

♦ Ethical considerations inherent in behavior management

Special education teachers are more than just teachers. They are required to fulfill numerous professional roles, including working with a wide range of professionals, paraprofessionals, and parents. The ability to work collaboratively is an essential skill for special education teachers. Nevertheless, their primary responsibility is for what goes on in the classroom. Consequently, special education teachers must be good decision-makers. They must be able to think critically about their effectiveness as teachers. Maintaining effective and functional relationships with all individuals involved in the special education process tends to benefit teaching effectiveness. Clear, direct, and accurate communication will protect your credibility and prevent a plethora of problems.

Professional roles, including

♦ Specific roles and responsibilities of teachers, for example:

- Teacher as a collaborator with
  — Other teachers
  — Teacher educators
  — Parents
  — Community groups
  — Outside agencies

- Teacher as a multidisciplinary team member

★ Who participates in an IEP meeting?

- Maintaining effective and efficient documentation

★ In a litigious age, documentation is a critical component of a special education teacher's responsibilities. How do you ensure accuracy and adequacy of documentation?

- Selecting appropriate environments and services for students

★ How will you define the least restrictive environment (LRE) for each individual student? What types of conflicts may be involved in determining the LRE?

- Critical evaluation and use of professional literature and organizations

- Reflecting on one's own teaching

- Teacher's role in a variety of teaching settings (self-contained classroom, resource room, itinerant, co-teacher in inclusion setting, etc.)

- Maintaining student confidentiality

★ With whom can you discuss your students?

★ What can you discuss?

★ What is a "mandated reporter"? When do you become one?

▸ Influence of teacher attitudes, values and behaviors on the learning of exceptional students

★ How might personal cultural biases affect one's teaching? What can one do to counteract them?

▸ Communicating with parents, guardians and appropriate community collaborators, for example:

  - directing parents and guardians to parent-educators or to other groups and resources

★ Educators increasingly recognize that actively including parents in decision-making processes provides a number of benefits. When possible, the student should be an active participant as well. What are some effective methods of maintaining communication with parents?

- Writing reports directly to parents

- Meeting with parents to discuss student concerns, progress, and IEP's

- Encouraging parent participation

★ What resources in your community assist parents of children with special needs? Local affiliates of CEC, LDA, ARC, CHADD and others are in place in many communities. If no such group exists, could you develop a support group?

  - Reciprocal communication and training with other service providers

★ What can you do to make parents feel more comfortable at IEP meetings?

Chapter 4

Don't be Defeated by
Multiple-Choice Questions

▶ ▶ ▶ ▶ ▶ ▶ ▶ ▶ ▶ ▶ ▶ ▶

Why the Multiple-Choice Tests Take Time

When you take the practice questions, you will see that there are very few simple identification questions of the "Which of the following is a kind of visual impairment?" sort. When The Praxis Series™ Assessments were first being developed by teachers and teacher educators across the country, it was almost universally agreed that prospective teachers should be able to analyze situations, synthesize material, and apply knowledge to specific examples. In short, they should be able to think as well as to recall specific facts, figures, or formulas. Consequently, you will find that you are being asked to think and to solve problems on your test. Such activity takes more time than simply answering identification questions.

In addition, questions that require you to analyze situations, synthesize material, and apply knowledge are usually longer than are simple identification questions. The Praxis Series test questions often present you with something to read (a case study, a sample of student work, a chart or graph) and ask you questions based on your reading. Strong reading skills are required, and you must read carefully. Both on this test and as a teacher, you will need to process and use what you read efficiently.

If you know that your reading skills are not strong, you may want to take a reading course. College campuses have reading labs that can help you strengthen your reading skills.

Understanding Multiple-Choice Questions

You will probably notice that the word order (or syntax) in multiple-choice questions is different from the word order you're used to seeing in ordinary things you read, like newspapers or textbooks. One of the reasons for this difference is that many such questions contain the phrase "which of the following."

The purpose of the phrase "which of the following" is to limit your choice of answers only to the list given. For example, look at this question.

> Which of the following is a flavor made from beans?
>
> (A) Strawberry
>
> (B) Cherry
>
> (C) Vanilla
>
> (D) Mint

You may know that chocolate and coffee are flavors made from beans also. But they are not listed, and the question asks you to select from among the list that follows ("which of the following"). So the answer has to be the only bean-derived flavor in the list: vanilla.

Notice that the answer can be substituted for the phrase "which of the following." In the question above, you could insert "vanilla" for "which of the following" and have the sentence "Vanilla is a flavor made from beans." Sometimes it helps to cross out "which of the following" and insert the various choices. You may want to give this technique a try as you answer various multiple-choice questions in the practice test.

Also, looking carefully at the "which of the following" phrase helps you to focus on what the question is asking you to find and on the answer choices. In the simple example above, all of the answer choices are flavors. Your job is to decide which of the flavors is the one made from beans.

The vanilla bean question is pretty straightforward. But the phrase "which of the following" can also be found in more challenging questions. Look at this question:

> Which of the following is a factor that impedes researchers' attempts to determine with certainty the prevalence of learning disabilities in the United States?
>
> (A) The absence of any definition of learning disabilities in federal guidelines for special education
>
> (B) A general reluctance on the part of educators and diagnosticians to classify students as having learning disabilities
>
> (C) The overlap in identification criteria between the classifications of severe learning disabilities and severe emotional disturbance
>
> (D) The lack of a precisely defined cut-off point at which a learning problem requiring remediation becomes a disability requiring special education

The placement of "which of the following" tells you that the list of choices is a list of factors that impede "researchers' attempts to determine with certainty the prevalence of learning disabilities in the United States." What are you supposed to find as an answer? You are supposed to find the choice that includes the factor that actually impedes researchers' attempts.

Sometimes it helps to put the question in your own words. Here, you could paraphrase the question as "When researchers attempt to determine the prevalence of learning disabilities, what stops them?" Definitions of learning disabilities are often imprecise in specifying the point at which a specific learning problem should be classified as a disability, and this factor affects identification of the condition. Therefore the correct answer is (D).

You may find that it helps to circle or underline each of the critical details of the question in your test book so that you don't miss any of them. It's only by looking at all parts of the question carefully that you will have all of the information you need to answer the question.

Circle or underline the critical parts of what is being asked in this question.

> Which of the following best describes an ecological inventory?
>
> (A) An analysis of the curriculum of a given school system
>
> (B) A compilation of specific behavioral management needs of a child with disabilities
>
> (C) A compilation of life skills needed by a child with disabilities in present or future settings
>
> (D) A synthesis of the past educational achievements of a child with disabilities

Here is one possible way you may have annotated the question:

> Which of the following best describes an ecological inventory?
>
> (A) An analysis of the curriculum of a given school system
>
> (B) A compilation of specific behavioral management needs of a child with disabilities
>
> (C) A compilation of life skills needed by a child with disabilities in present or future settings
>
> (D) A synthesis of the past educational achievements of a child with disabilities

After spending a minute with the question, you can probably see that you are being asked to define what an ecological inventory is. An ecological inventory is designed to determine those skills needed by a particular individual in his or her current and future environment. The correct answer is (C).

The important thing is understanding what the question is asking. With enough practice, you should be able to determine what any question is asking. Knowing the answer is, of course, a different matter, but you have to understand a question before you can answer it.

It takes more work to understand "which of the following" questions when there are even more words in a question. Questions that require application or interpretation invariably require extra reading.

Consider this question.

> Brian, a high school student with a learning disability, receives resource-room instruction in English. Brian's parents have requested a conference with the resource-room teacher two months after the start of the school year to discuss his progress in writing. Which of the following would be the most appropriate item for the teacher's agenda for this meeting?
>
> (A) Ask the parents to compare Brian's written work with that of another student.
>
> (B) Ask the parents to propose new instructional objectives for the written-expression section of Brian's individualized education plan (IEP).
>
> (C) Offer a comparison of Brian's recent grades on writing assignments with his achievement-test scores from the previous year.
>
> (D) Show the parents a folder of Brian's written work and discuss apparent strengths and weaknesses.

Being able to select the right answer, (D), depends on your understanding of the goals of the conference with Brian's parents. Of the choices given, discussing examples of Brian's work best addresses the purposes of the meeting. Asking parents to compare their child's work with that of another student, as in option (A), is not appropriate. (B) is not correct because this is not an IEP meeting, and because, while the parents have input into their child's IEP, it is not appropriate for the teacher to ask parents to propose objectives. (C) is not correct because the comparison it suggests is unlikely to be informative.

Understanding Questions Containing "NOT," "LEAST," "EXCEPT"

In addition to "which of the following" and details that must be understood, the words "NOT," "EXCEPT," and "LEAST" often make comprehension of test questions more difficult. These words are always capitalized when they appear in The Praxis Series test questions, but they are easily (and frequently) overlooked.

For the following test question, determine what kind of answer you're looking for and what the details of the question are.

> Computer-assisted instruction has been shown to be an important teaching method for students with mental retardation for all of the following reasons EXCEPT:
>
> (A) The computer requires little teacher intervention, freeing the teacher to prepare upcoming lessons.
>
> (B) The computer can be programmed to deliver immediate feedback on the correctness of a response.
>
> (C) The computer can be programmed to provide as much repetition as a student needs.
>
> (D) Computer graphics and sound can maintain a student's motivation and attention to task.

You're looking for a reason that does NOT explain why computer-assisted instruction is useful for students with mental retardation. The correct answer is (A), because all of the other choices are good reasons for using computer-assisted instruction for these students. (A) is false because

effective computer-assisted instruction tends to require as much teacher monitoring and intervention as other types of individualized student work.

TIP It's easy to get confused while you're processing the information to answer a question with a LEAST, NOT, or EXCEPT in the question. If you treat the word "LEAST," "NOT," or "EXCEPT" as one of the details you must satisfy, you have a better chance of understanding what the question is asking. And when you check your answer, make "LEAST," "NOT," or "EXCEPT" one of the details you check for.

Understanding Questions Based on Case Studies

Case studies contain a body of introductory material followed by a group of related questions. Questions based on a case study require a careful strategy that balances time, efficiency, and critical understanding.

Since the case study can often be dense and complex, you should read through the description of the situation before reading the questions, but you should not spend time taking notes or reading the situation multiple times until you know what the questions are asking you to do.

For example, you might encounter a case study like this:

> Michelle, a 19 year old whose parents are deceased, has profound mental retardation and lives in a group home. She is bused to a special class by the local school district. Michelle has had frequent, extended absences from school because of her frail physical condition.

She is nonambulatory and nonverbal; her vision and hearing are intact. She can communicate a few basic needs by means of a pictorial language board.

In your first reading, you should make sure that you understand the basics. In this example, you should grasp that Michelle has profound mental retardation and is nonambulatory and nonverbal, and that her parents are not living. In this first reading, you should also anticipate being asked questions about appropriate curriculum and methods for Michelle. Once you have gained an overall understanding of the case, you should answer the first question.

> Which of the following is the appropriate focus of Michelle's individualized education plan (IEP)?
>
> (A) Functional academics
>
> (B) Self-care skills
>
> (C) Basic academic skills
>
> (D) Prevocational skills

For the second question, you need to focus on the status of Michelle's parents.

> Since Michelle's parents are deceased, who is required to review and approve her educational program?
>
> (A) A representative of the state agency for children's services
>
> (B) A court-designated staff member of the group home in which she resides
>
> (C) A surrogate parent appointed by the local education agency
>
> (D) A blood relative willing to assume this responsibility

The correct answers to these two questions are (B) and (C), respectively.

Be Familiar with Multiple-Choice Question Types

Now that you have reviewed the basics of succeeding at multiple-choice questions, it should help to review the most common question formats you are likely to see.

1. Complete the statement

In this type of question, you are given an incomplete statement. You must select the choice that will make the completed statement correct.

> According to the Individuals with Disabilities Education Act (IDEA), when parents and schools disagree over educational issues for a child with a disability, either party can request a
>
> (A) mediator
>
> (B) due-process hearing
>
> (C) new teacher for the student
>
> (D) court date

To check your answer, reread the question and add your answer choice at the end. Be sure that your choice best completes the sentence. The correct answer is (B).

2. Which of the following

This question type is discussed in detail in a previous section. The question contains the details that must be satisfied for a correct answer, and it uses "which of the following" to limit the choices to the four choices shown, as this example demonstrates.

Which of the following is most clearly an example of a student using inappropriate syntax?

(A) Saying, "I see football game"

(B) Saying "Wa wa" as a substitute for "Water"

(C) Saying, "Me sister shoes new happy"

(D) Saying, "He drinked his milk"

The correct answer is (C).

3. Roman numeral choices

This format is used when there can be more than one correct answer in the list. Consider the following example.

Under the Individuals with Disabilities Education Act (IDEA), which of the following criteria must be met before a student is classified as severely emotionally disturbed?

I. The condition must be observed over a long period of time.

II. The condition must adversely affect the student's educational performance.

III. The student must previously have been diagnosed as socially maladjusted.

(A) I only

(B) I and II only

(C) II and III only

(D) I, II, and III

One useful strategy in this type of question is to assess each possible answer before looking at the answer choices and then evaluate the answer choices. In the question above, Statement I is correct because federal law specifies that the characteristics must be observed over a long period

of time. Statement II is also correct, because federal law specifies that the characteristics must be present to a marked degree and adversely affect educational performance. Statement III is clearly incorrect because federal law does not require that the student previously be diagnosed as socially maladjusted. Therefore, the correct answer is (B).

4. Questions containing LEAST, EXCEPT, NOT

This question type is discussed at length above. It asks you to select the choice that doesn't fit. You must be very careful with this question type, because it's easy to forget that you're selecting the negative. This question type is used in situations in which there are several good solutions, or ways to approach something, but also a clearly wrong way to do something.

5. Other Formats

New formats are developed from time to time in order to find new ways of assessing knowledge with multiple-choice questions. If you see a format you are not familiar with, read the directions carefully. Then read and approach the question the way you would any other question, asking yourself what you are supposed to be looking for, and what details are given in the question that help you find the answer.

Useful Facts about the Tests

1. **You can answer the questions in any order.** You can go through the questions from beginning to end, as many test takers do, or you can create your own path. Perhaps you will want to answer questions in your strongest field first and then move from your strengths to your weaker areas. There is no right or wrong way. Use the approach that works for you.

2. **There are no trick questions on the tests.** You don't have to find any hidden meanings or worry about trick wording. All of the questions on the tests ask about subject matter knowledge in a straightforward manner.

3. **Don't worry about answer patterns.** There is one myth that says that answers on multiple-choice tests follow patterns. There is another myth that there will never be more than two questions with the same lettered answer following each other. There is no truth to either of these myths. Select the answer you think is correct, based on your knowledge of the subject.

4. **There is no penalty for guessing.** Your test score is based on the number of correct answers you have, and incorrect answers are not counted against you. When you don't know the answer to a question, try to eliminate any obviously wrong answers and then guess at the correct one.

5. **It's OK to write in your test booklet.** You can work problems right on the pages of the booklet, make notes to yourself, mark questions you want to review later, or write anything at all. Your test booklet will be destroyed after you are finished with it, so use it in any way that is helpful to you.

Smart Tips for Taking the Test

1. **Put your answers in the right "bubbles."** It seems obvious, but be sure that you are "bubbling in" the answer to the right question on your answer sheet. You would be surprised at how many candidates fill in a "bubble" without checking to see that the number matches the question they are answering.

2. **Skip the questions you find to be extremely difficult.** There are bound to be some questions that you think are hard. Rather than trying to answer these on your first pass through the test, leave them blank and mark them in your test booklet so that you can come back to them. Pay attention to the time as you answer the rest of the questions on the test and try to finish with 10 or 15 minutes remaining so that you can go back over the questions you left blank. Even if you don't know the answer the second time you read the questions, see whether you can narrow down the possible answers, and then guess.

3. **Keep track of the time.** Bring a watch to the test, just in case the clock in the test room is difficult for you to see. Remember that, on average, you have about one minute to answer each of the questions. One minute may not seem like much time, but you will be able to answer a number of questions in only a few seconds each. You will probably have plenty of time to answer all of the questions, but if you find yourself becoming bogged down in one section, you might decide to move on and come back to that section later.

4. **Read all of the possible answers before selecting one** — and then reread the question to be sure the answer you have selected really answers the question being asked. Remember that a question that contains a phrase like "Which of the following does NOT. . ." is asking for the one answer that is NOT a correct statement or conclusion.

5. **Check your answers.** If you have extra time left over at the end of the test, look over each question and make sure that you have filled in the "bubble" on the answer sheet as you intended. Many candidates make careless mistakes that could have been corrected if they had checked their answers.

6. **Don't worry about your score when you are taking the test.** No one is expected to get all of the questions correct. Your score on this test is not analogous to your score on the SAT, the GRE, or other similar tests. It doesn't matter on this test whether you score very high or barely pass. If you meet the minimum passing scores for your state and you meet the other requirements of the state for obtaining a teaching license, you will receive a license. Your actual score doesn't matter, as long as it is above the minimum required score. With your score report you will receive a booklet entitled *Understanding Your Praxis Scores,* which lists the passing scores for your state.

Chapter 5

Practice Questions for the *Special Education: Core Knowledge* Tests

▶   ▶   ▶   ▶   ▶   ▶   ▶   ▶   ▶   ▶   ▶   ▶

Practice Questions

Now that you have studied the content topics and have worked through strategies relating to multiple-choice questions, you should take the following practice test. You will probably find it helpful to simulate actual testing conditions, giving yourself about 60 minutes to work on the questions. You can cut out and use the answer sheet provided if you wish.

Keep in mind that the test you take at an actual administration will have different questions, although the proportion of questions in each area and major subarea will be approximately the same. You should not expect the percentage of questions you answer correctly in these practice questions to be exactly the same as when you take the test at an actual administration, since numerous factors affect a person's performance in any given testing situation.

When you have finished the practice questions, you can score your answers and read the explanations of the best answer choices in chapter 6.

THE **PRAXIS**
S E R I E S
Professional Assessments for Beginning Teachers ®

TEST CODE:

TEST NAME:
Special Education:
Core Knowledge

Practice Questions

Time—60 Minutes
60 Questions

(Note, at the official administration of test 0350, there will be 150 questions, and you will be allowed 120 minutes to complete the test; for test 0352, there will be 50 questions, and you will be allowed 60 minutes to complete the test; for tests 0351 and 0353, there will be 60 questions, and you will be allowed 60 minutes to complete the test.)

DO NOT USE INK

Use only a pencil with soft black lead (No. 2 or HB) to complete this answer sheet.
Be sure to fill in completely the oval that corresponds to the proper letter or number.
Completely erase any errors or stray marks.

THE PRAXIS SERIES
Professional Assessments for Beginning Teachers®

Answer Sheet C

PAGE 1

1. NAME
Enter your last name and first initial.
Omit spaces, hyphens, apostrophes, etc.

Last Name (first 6 letters) F I

2.

YOUR NAME: (Print)

Last Name (Family or Surname) — First Name (Given) — M. I.

MAILING ADDRESS: (Print)

P.O. Box or Street Address

Apt. # (If any)

City — State or Province

Country — Zip or Postal Code

TELEPHONE NUMBER: ( ) Home — ( ) Business

SIGNATURE: — **TEST DATE:**

3. DATE OF BIRTH
Month | Day

Jan.
Feb.
Mar.
April
May
June
July
Aug.
Sept.
Oct.
Nov.
Dec.

4. SOCIAL SECURITY NUMBER

5. CANDIDATE ID NUMBER

6. TEST CENTER / REPORTING LOCATION

Center Number — Room Number

Center Name

City — State or Province

Country

7. TEST CODE / FORM CODE

8. TEST BOOK SERIAL NUMBER

9. TEST FORM

10. TEST NAME

Educational Testing Service, ETS, the ETS logo, and THE PRAXIS SERIES;PROFESSIONAL ASSESSMENTS FOR BEGINNING TEACHERS and its logo are registered trademarks of Educational Testing Service.

ETS Educational Testing Service

51055 • 08920 • TF71M500
MH01159   Q2573-06

I.N. 202974

1 2 3 4

CERTIFICATION STATEMENT: (Please write the following statement below. DO NOT PRINT.)

"I hereby agree to the conditions set forth in the *Registration Bulletin* and certify that I am the person whose name and address appear on this answer sheet."

_____

_____

_____

SIGNATURE: _____   DATE: _____/_____/_____

Month   Day   Year

BE SURE EACH MARK IS DARK AND COMPLETELY FILLS THE INTENDED SPACE AS ILLUSTRATED HERE: ● .

1 Ⓐ Ⓑ Ⓒ Ⓓ	41 Ⓐ Ⓑ Ⓒ Ⓓ	81 Ⓐ Ⓑ Ⓒ Ⓓ	121 Ⓐ Ⓑ Ⓒ Ⓓ
2 Ⓐ Ⓑ Ⓒ Ⓓ	42 Ⓐ Ⓑ Ⓒ Ⓓ	82 Ⓐ Ⓑ Ⓒ Ⓓ	122 Ⓐ Ⓑ Ⓒ Ⓓ
3 Ⓐ Ⓑ Ⓒ Ⓓ	43 Ⓐ Ⓑ Ⓒ Ⓓ	83 Ⓐ Ⓑ Ⓒ Ⓓ	123 Ⓐ Ⓑ Ⓒ Ⓓ
4 Ⓐ Ⓑ Ⓒ Ⓓ	44 Ⓐ Ⓑ Ⓒ Ⓓ	84 Ⓐ Ⓑ Ⓒ Ⓓ	124 Ⓐ Ⓑ Ⓒ Ⓓ
5 Ⓐ Ⓑ Ⓒ Ⓓ	45 Ⓐ Ⓑ Ⓒ Ⓓ	85 Ⓐ Ⓑ Ⓒ Ⓓ	125 Ⓐ Ⓑ Ⓒ Ⓓ
6 Ⓐ Ⓑ Ⓒ Ⓓ	46 Ⓐ Ⓑ Ⓒ Ⓓ	86 Ⓐ Ⓑ Ⓒ Ⓓ	126 Ⓐ Ⓑ Ⓒ Ⓓ
7 Ⓐ Ⓑ Ⓒ Ⓓ	47 Ⓐ Ⓑ Ⓒ Ⓓ	87 Ⓐ Ⓑ Ⓒ Ⓓ	127 Ⓐ Ⓑ Ⓒ Ⓓ
8 Ⓐ Ⓑ Ⓒ Ⓓ	48 Ⓐ Ⓑ Ⓒ Ⓓ	88 Ⓐ Ⓑ Ⓒ Ⓓ	128 Ⓐ Ⓑ Ⓒ Ⓓ
9 Ⓐ Ⓑ Ⓒ Ⓓ	49 Ⓐ Ⓑ Ⓒ Ⓓ	89 Ⓐ Ⓑ Ⓒ Ⓓ	129 Ⓐ Ⓑ Ⓒ Ⓓ
10 Ⓐ Ⓑ Ⓒ Ⓓ	50 Ⓐ Ⓑ Ⓒ Ⓓ	90 Ⓐ Ⓑ Ⓒ Ⓓ	130 Ⓐ Ⓑ Ⓒ Ⓓ
11 Ⓐ Ⓑ Ⓒ Ⓓ	51 Ⓐ Ⓑ Ⓒ Ⓓ	91 Ⓐ Ⓑ Ⓒ Ⓓ	131 Ⓐ Ⓑ Ⓒ Ⓓ
12 Ⓐ Ⓑ Ⓒ Ⓓ	52 Ⓐ Ⓑ Ⓒ Ⓓ	92 Ⓐ Ⓑ Ⓒ Ⓓ	132 Ⓐ Ⓑ Ⓒ Ⓓ
13 Ⓐ Ⓑ Ⓒ Ⓓ	53 Ⓐ Ⓑ Ⓒ Ⓓ	93 Ⓐ Ⓑ Ⓒ Ⓓ	133 Ⓐ Ⓑ Ⓒ Ⓓ
14 Ⓐ Ⓑ Ⓒ Ⓓ	54 Ⓐ Ⓑ Ⓒ Ⓓ	94 Ⓐ Ⓑ Ⓒ Ⓓ	134 Ⓐ Ⓑ Ⓒ Ⓓ
15 Ⓐ Ⓑ Ⓒ Ⓓ	55 Ⓐ Ⓑ Ⓒ Ⓓ	95 Ⓐ Ⓑ Ⓒ Ⓓ	135 Ⓐ Ⓑ Ⓒ Ⓓ
16 Ⓐ Ⓑ Ⓒ Ⓓ	56 Ⓐ Ⓑ Ⓒ Ⓓ	96 Ⓐ Ⓑ Ⓒ Ⓓ	136 Ⓐ Ⓑ Ⓒ Ⓓ
17 Ⓐ Ⓑ Ⓒ Ⓓ	57 Ⓐ Ⓑ Ⓒ Ⓓ	97 Ⓐ Ⓑ Ⓒ Ⓓ	137 Ⓐ Ⓑ Ⓒ Ⓓ
18 Ⓐ Ⓑ Ⓒ Ⓓ	58 Ⓐ Ⓑ Ⓒ Ⓓ	98 Ⓐ Ⓑ Ⓒ Ⓓ	138 Ⓐ Ⓑ Ⓒ Ⓓ
19 Ⓐ Ⓑ Ⓒ Ⓓ	59 Ⓐ Ⓑ Ⓒ Ⓓ	99 Ⓐ Ⓑ Ⓒ Ⓓ	139 Ⓐ Ⓑ Ⓒ Ⓓ
20 Ⓐ Ⓑ Ⓒ Ⓓ	60 Ⓐ Ⓑ Ⓒ Ⓓ	100 Ⓐ Ⓑ Ⓒ Ⓓ	140 Ⓐ Ⓑ Ⓒ Ⓓ
21 Ⓐ Ⓑ Ⓒ Ⓓ	61 Ⓐ Ⓑ Ⓒ Ⓓ	101 Ⓐ Ⓑ Ⓒ Ⓓ	141 Ⓐ Ⓑ Ⓒ Ⓓ
22 Ⓐ Ⓑ Ⓒ Ⓓ	62 Ⓐ Ⓑ Ⓒ Ⓓ	102 Ⓐ Ⓑ Ⓒ Ⓓ	142 Ⓐ Ⓑ Ⓒ Ⓓ
23 Ⓐ Ⓑ Ⓒ Ⓓ	63 Ⓐ Ⓑ Ⓒ Ⓓ	103 Ⓐ Ⓑ Ⓒ Ⓓ	143 Ⓐ Ⓑ Ⓒ Ⓓ
24 Ⓐ Ⓑ Ⓒ Ⓓ	64 Ⓐ Ⓑ Ⓒ Ⓓ	104 Ⓐ Ⓑ Ⓒ Ⓓ	144 Ⓐ Ⓑ Ⓒ Ⓓ
25 Ⓐ Ⓑ Ⓒ Ⓓ	65 Ⓐ Ⓑ Ⓒ Ⓓ	105 Ⓐ Ⓑ Ⓒ Ⓓ	145 Ⓐ Ⓑ Ⓒ Ⓓ
26 Ⓐ Ⓑ Ⓒ Ⓓ	66 Ⓐ Ⓑ Ⓒ Ⓓ	106 Ⓐ Ⓑ Ⓒ Ⓓ	146 Ⓐ Ⓑ Ⓒ Ⓓ
27 Ⓐ Ⓑ Ⓒ Ⓓ	67 Ⓐ Ⓑ Ⓒ Ⓓ	107 Ⓐ Ⓑ Ⓒ Ⓓ	147 Ⓐ Ⓑ Ⓒ Ⓓ
28 Ⓐ Ⓑ Ⓒ Ⓓ	68 Ⓐ Ⓑ Ⓒ Ⓓ	108 Ⓐ Ⓑ Ⓒ Ⓓ	148 Ⓐ Ⓑ Ⓒ Ⓓ
29 Ⓐ Ⓑ Ⓒ Ⓓ	69 Ⓐ Ⓑ Ⓒ Ⓓ	109 Ⓐ Ⓑ Ⓒ Ⓓ	149 Ⓐ Ⓑ Ⓒ Ⓓ
30 Ⓐ Ⓑ Ⓒ Ⓓ	70 Ⓐ Ⓑ Ⓒ Ⓓ	110 Ⓐ Ⓑ Ⓒ Ⓓ	150 Ⓐ Ⓑ Ⓒ Ⓓ
31 Ⓐ Ⓑ Ⓒ Ⓓ	71 Ⓐ Ⓑ Ⓒ Ⓓ	111 Ⓐ Ⓑ Ⓒ Ⓓ	151 Ⓐ Ⓑ Ⓒ Ⓓ
32 Ⓐ Ⓑ Ⓒ Ⓓ	72 Ⓐ Ⓑ Ⓒ Ⓓ	112 Ⓐ Ⓑ Ⓒ Ⓓ	152 Ⓐ Ⓑ Ⓒ Ⓓ
33 Ⓐ Ⓑ Ⓒ Ⓓ	73 Ⓐ Ⓑ Ⓒ Ⓓ	113 Ⓐ Ⓑ Ⓒ Ⓓ	153 Ⓐ Ⓑ Ⓒ Ⓓ
34 Ⓐ Ⓑ Ⓒ Ⓓ	74 Ⓐ Ⓑ Ⓒ Ⓓ	114 Ⓐ Ⓑ Ⓒ Ⓓ	154 Ⓐ Ⓑ Ⓒ Ⓓ
35 Ⓐ Ⓑ Ⓒ Ⓓ	75 Ⓐ Ⓑ Ⓒ Ⓓ	115 Ⓐ Ⓑ Ⓒ Ⓓ	155 Ⓐ Ⓑ Ⓒ Ⓓ
36 Ⓐ Ⓑ Ⓒ Ⓓ	76 Ⓐ Ⓑ Ⓒ Ⓓ	116 Ⓐ Ⓑ Ⓒ Ⓓ	156 Ⓐ Ⓑ Ⓒ Ⓓ
37 Ⓐ Ⓑ Ⓒ Ⓓ	77 Ⓐ Ⓑ Ⓒ Ⓓ	117 Ⓐ Ⓑ Ⓒ Ⓓ	157 Ⓐ Ⓑ Ⓒ Ⓓ
38 Ⓐ Ⓑ Ⓒ Ⓓ	78 Ⓐ Ⓑ Ⓒ Ⓓ	118 Ⓐ Ⓑ Ⓒ Ⓓ	158 Ⓐ Ⓑ Ⓒ Ⓓ
39 Ⓐ Ⓑ Ⓒ Ⓓ	79 Ⓐ Ⓑ Ⓒ Ⓓ	119 Ⓐ Ⓑ Ⓒ Ⓓ	159 Ⓐ Ⓑ Ⓒ Ⓓ
40 Ⓐ Ⓑ Ⓒ Ⓓ	80 Ⓐ Ⓑ Ⓒ Ⓓ	120 Ⓐ Ⓑ Ⓒ Ⓓ	160 Ⓐ Ⓑ Ⓒ Ⓓ

FOR ETS USE ONLY	R1	R2	R3	R4	R5	R6	R7	R8	TR	CS

SPECIAL EDUCATION: CORE KNOWLEDGE

1. In making decisions about curriculum and instruction for a student with a disability, which of the following types of information is generally the most useful?

    (A) Scores from standardized tests
    (B) The category of the disability
    (C) Curriculum-based assessment
    (D) The amount of time the student spends in the resource room

2. Randi is a 12 year old who scores within the average range for her age on the Woodcock-Johnson Cognitive Battery but is significantly below grade level in reading and writing, and at grade level in math. This profile is most consistent with a possible diagnosis of

    (A) mild mental retardation
    (B) specific learning disability
    (C) attention-deficit disorder
    (D) autism

3. IDEA '97 requires which of the following on an individualized education plan (IEP)?

    (A) A statement that explains why the placement is the least-restrictive environment
    (B) A multiyear outline of instructional objectives
    (C) A guarantee that the student will achieve the goals of the IEP
    (D) A budget for the services the student will receive

4. Which of the following is NOT a characteristic of effective inclusive schools?

    (A) Collaboration among professionals
    (B) A philosophy that celebrates diversity
    (C) Use of cooperative learning
    (D) An emphasis on categorical placement of students with disabilities

5. "Filling out applications," "after-school job working with electrician," and "tutoring in functional reading skills" are all activities listed on Jeff's individualized transition plan (ITP). Jeff's long-term goal is most likely to

    (A) attend a four-year college
    (B) obtain skilled or semiskilled employment
    (C) live in a group home
    (D) work in a sheltered workshop

6. Mobility training for students who are visually impaired can involve all of the following devices EXCEPT

    (A) a Mowat sensor
    (B) a laser cane
    (C) a sonic guide
    (D) an Optacon scanner

7. Two tests that could be used to identify a student as having mental retardation are

    (A) WISC-III and WJ Tests of Achievement
    (B) WJ Cognitive Battery and WJ Tests of Achievement
    (C) MMPI and Meyers-Briggs
    (D) Stanford-Binet and Scales of Independent Behavior

8. The most frequently occurring permanently disabling birth defect, characterized by an abnormal opening in the spinal column, is called

   (A) spina bifida
   (B) cerebral palsy
   (C) muscular dystrophy
   (D) multiple sclerosis

9. A curriculum that focuses on teaching functional and independent living skills, utilizes augmentative communication and assistive technology, and provides for extensive support in the classroom is most likely used with students with

   (A) learning disabilities
   (B) multiple and severe disabilities
   (C) emotional or behavioral disorders
   (D) attention-deficit/hyperactivity disorder

10. *Diana* v. *State Board of Education*, 1970, *Larry P.* v. *Riles*, 1972, and *Lau* v. *Nichols*, 1974, influenced the drafting of the Individuals with Disabilities Education Act (IDEA) and addressed the issue of

    (A) zero reject
    (B) expulsions
    (C) nondiscriminatory assessment
    (D) out-of-state schooling

11. In order to identify a student with learning disabilities, most examiners are concerned with a discrepancy between

    (A) ability and achievement tests, with ability being higher than achievement
    (B) ability and achievement tests, with achievement being higher than ability
    (C) curriculum-based assessment (CBA) and achievement tests, with CBA being higher than achievement
    (D) CBA and achievement tests, with achievement being higher than CBA

12. IDEA '97 contains all the following provisions EXCEPT

    (A) nondiscriminatory testing
    (B) IEP's for college students 21 or younger
    (C) education in the least-restrictive environment
    (D) mandated transition planning

13. On the basis of cases such as *Hudson* v. *Rowley* (1982), the courts have determined that "appropriate education" means that

    (A) students will have all the resources and related services needed to fulfill their potential
    (B) services that maximize achievement will be provided as long as the cost is not prohibitive
    (C) learners with disabilities will have the opportunity to achieve commensurate with peers
    (D) interpreters will be provided for all deaf students

14. In a full-inclusion model, services to students with disabilities are available in

    (A) general-education classrooms
    (B) resource rooms
    (C) self-contained classrooms
    (D) special schools

15. From a *functional* perspective, deafness is related to difficulties with the ability to

    (A) hear sounds
    (B) hear and understand speech
    (C) read lips
    (D) hear frequencies above 10,000 Hz

16. Many students with disabilities receive instruction in social skills because

    (A) social skills are crucial for successful inclusive education
    (B) they are unable to benefit from educational training
    (C) teachers in general education focus primarily on social skills instruction
    (D) social skills are easier to teach than academic skills

17. According to a behavioral classroom management model, if a student exhibits an inappropriate behavior, the teacher should

    (A) reinforce the inappropriate behavior
    (B) reinforce an appropriate but incompatible behavior
    (C) negatively reinforce the inappropriate behavior
    (D) talk about the reasons for the problem with the student

18. Which of the following is true about a full-inclusion program?

    (A) The student spends part of the day in the general education classroom and part in the resource room.
    (B) The student spends the entire day in the resource room.
    (C) The student does not need any support services.
    (D) The general education teacher and special education teacher share the responsibility for the student's education.

19. Shania is a student with learning disabilities in the tenth grade. Because her reading level is low, she receives direct instruction in decoding skills to facilitate recognition of high-frequency words. Shania's instruction represents a

    (A) remedial approach
    (B) compensatory approach
    (C) holistic approach
    (D) learning modality approach

20. The most likely reason for administering the entire Woodcock-Johnson Psychoeducational Battery, Third Edition, to a student would be in an evaluation for

    (A) mental retardation
    (B) learning disabilities
    (C) serious emotional disturbance
    (D) attention-deficit disorder

21. In order to meet the needs of an infant or toddler with disabilities, the results of an evaluation are used to develop an

    (A) IEP
    (B) IFSP
    (C) ITP
    (D) ISP

22. Which of the following instructional approaches does NOT involve student-to-student interaction?

    (A) Cooperative learning
    (B) Cross-age tutoring
    (C) Direct instruction
    (D) Study skills groups

23. Adapting existing vocal or gestural abilities; teaching manual signing, static symbols, or icons; and using technological devices for speech and language are all examples of

    (A) assistive technology
    (B) Blissymbols
    (C) synthesized speech
    (D) augmentative communication

24. Mitch is a college-bound high school senior with learning disabilities. His IEP indicates that he uses a tape recorder in his English class and a calculator for taking tests in Algebra 2. These accommodations are examples of

    (A) assistive technology
    (B) personal computing support
    (C) remediation
    (D) self-management

25. About 80 percent of all speech disorders are characterized by difficulties with

    (A) fluency
    (B) delayed speech onset
    (C) articulation
    (D) voice

26. Most people with severe and multiple disabilities have a primary condition of

    (A) emotional disturbance
    (B) cerebral palsy
    (C) sensory impairment
    (D) mental retardation

27. Students with mild mental retardation make up what percentage of all students identified with mental retardation?

    (A) 90%
    (B) 70%
    (C) 50%
    (D) Less than 50%

28. Using objectives from the student's work in class as a means to evaluate progress and adapt instruction is known as

    (A) curriculum-based assessment
    (B) standardized achievement testing
    (C) adaptive skill instruction
    (D) guided practice

29. All of the following are components of IDEA '97 EXCEPT:

    (A) Parents who believe the school's evaluation is inadequate may request an independent evaluation.
    (B) Autism is considered a specific disability category.
    (C) A student with a disability who brings drugs or weapons to school may be expelled.
    (D) ADD/ADHD is considered a specific disability category.

30. Placing students with the same disabilities together for instructional purposes represents a

    (A) categorical approach
    (B) cross-categorical approach
    (C) noncategorical approach
    (D) least-restrictive-environment approach

31. Bruce and Lou, who sit next to each other, distract each other in the classroom. The teacher has tried rewarding them for appropriate behavior, but their behavior has not changed. The teacher then changes their seating so that they are on opposite ends of the classroom. They now rarely distract each other. This is an example of

    (A) manipulating the consequent stimulus
    (B) manipulating the antecedent stimulus
    (C) ignoring inappropriate behavior
    (D) using the Premack principle

32. In order to be identified as having mental retardation, a child must demonstrate significantly subaverage intellectual functioning and

    (A) a discrepancy between ability and achievement
    (B) genetic abnormalities
    (C) seizure syndrome and brain dysfunction
    (D) related limitations on two or more areas of adaptive skills

33. Having students keep track of their own behavior and then receive rewards for appropriate behavior is known as

    (A) contingency-based self-management
    (B) functional assessment
    (C) reality therapy
    (D) ecological assessment

34. Which of the following would be most indicative of a receptive language disorder?

    (A) A student uses the same words and phrases over and over again in different situations.
    (B) A student hesitates before talking and rarely initiates conversation.
    (C) A student looks at other students to see what they are doing when directions are given.
    (D) A student cannot hear the teacher unless the teacher raises his or her voice.

35. A psychoanalytic approach would explain behavior disorders as resulting from

    (A) an individual's self-concept
    (B) learned inappropriate behaviors
    (C) neurological abnormalities
    (D) early traumatic experiences

36. A teacher who sets explicit and clear goals for each lesson, presents a logical sequence of tasks, gives clear directions on how to do each task, models the task, engages the student in guided practice, asks frequent questions, gives feedback, and does not move on to the next task until the student masters the one at hand is using

    (A) a metacognitive approach
    (B) diagnostic-prescriptive method
    (C) direct instruction
    (D) cooperative learning

37. A resource room teacher would be most likely to contact an occupational therapist for help with

    (A) counseling a high school student with learning disabilities about applying to college
    (B) teaching a student with muscular dystrophy how to paint with a brush
    (C) talking to parents about their genetic risk of producing a seriously ill infant
    (D) arranging a play-therapy group for young students with disabilities

38. Approximately two-thirds of children with attention deficit disorder or attention deficit hyperactivity disorder also have some kind of

    (A) conduct disorder
    (B) learning disability
    (C) mental retardation
    (D) tic or twitching

39. Students with learning disabilities account for approximately what percentage of the students in special education?

    (A) 5%
    (B) 10%
    (C) 33%
    (D) 50%

40. Cedric is a fourth grader who seems to be having difficulty keeping up with reading tasks. His parents are interested in looking into the possibility of special education services. They have made an appointment with Cedric's teacher and the special education teacher who works with fourth-grade students. The likely first step the school will take is

    (A) prereferral screening and in-class observation
    (B) formal testing and evaluation for learning disabilities
    (C) having the parents meet with the principal to discourage them from looking into special education services
    (D) ordering books-on-tape for all of Cedric's fourth-grade texts

41. Chelsea, a student with a mild hearing loss, often has difficulty following the teacher's directions in class, particularly when the teacher is doing work at the blackboard. Which of the following suggestions would be a most appropriate first step for the teacher to try to improve Chelsea's behavior?

    (A) Repeat all directions directly into Chelsea's ear.
    (B) Do not give directions when facing the board.
    (C) Provide an interpreter for Chelsea.
    (D) Have another student write down all assignments for Chelsea.

42. Nicky is a fifth-grade student. On an informal reading inventory, his independent grade-reading level was 3.0, his instructional level was 3.7, and his frustration level was 4.2. Which of the following is the most sensible advice for a special education teacher to give to Nicky's social studies teacher?

    (A) Continue to use fifth-grade reading material, which will force Nicky to catch up.
    (B) Try to find and use content-appropriate reading at a fourth-grade level.
    (C) Try to find and use content-appropriate reading at a third-grade level.
    (D) Excuse Nicky from social studies reading.

43. Roberto, who speaks English as a second language, has been having difficulty with reading and writing tasks in his third-grade class. After he is referred for testing, his scores on the WISC-III are significantly subaverage. His family contests the results of the testing. Which of the following principles from IDEA '97 can they cite as inconsistent with the test?

    (A) Zero reject
    (B) Nondiscriminatory assessment
    (C) Parent participation
    (D) Individualized education

44. Which of the following would be an appropriate functional writing unit for high school students with mild mental retardation?

    (A) Systematic practice in cursive writing
    (B) Learning to fill out applications for college
    (C) Learning to fill out job applications
    (D) Learning to spell basic sight words

45. All of the following methods are designed to decrease or extinguish behavior EXCEPT

    (A) ignoring the target behavior
    (B) cost response for the target behavior
    (C) punishment of the target behavior
    (D) negative reinforcement of the target behavior

46. Which of the following perspectives attributes emotional and behavioral disorders to poor interaction with the environment, in which the student and the environment affect each other reciprocally, and often advocates interventions that involve altering the entire social system?

    (A) Behavioral
    (B) Ecological
    (C) Humanistic
    (D) Psychoanalytic

47. Requiring all members of a group to achieve a certain goal before any member of the group receives an award is an example of

    (A) group-contingency contracting
    (B) operant conditioning
    (C) response cost
    (D) cognitive behavior modification

48. The Vineland Adaptive Behavior Scales would most likely be used in the diagnosis of

    (A) gifted and talented
    (B) learning disabilities
    (C) mental retardation
    (D) fragile X syndrome

49. Planning that includes goals and objectives addressing future employment, independent living, adult services, and community participation for students 14 years and older with disabilities is known as

    (A) an individualized education plan (IEP)
    (B) an individualized transition plan (ITP)
    (C) an individualized family service plan (IFSP)
    (D) a regular education initiative (REI)

50. Tim is a student with a behavior disorder who talks back to his teacher so much that he consistently disrupts the rest of the class. The teacher has asked the administration to suspend Tim for several days. The administration responds that it will not suspend Tim because his behavior is connected to his disability. Suspending him would be discriminating against Tim on the basis of his disability. The principle of IDEA '97 that supports the administration's decision is

    (A) due process
    (B) nondiscriminatory assessment
    (C) parental participation
    (D) zero reject

51. The approach to reading instruction that uses students' language and experiences and in which reading is taught as a meaning-oriented, integrated activity rather than as a collection of separate skills is called

    (A) whole language
    (B) phonics
    (C) linguistic
    (D) basal

52. Which principle of IDEA '97 requires including students with disabilities in general education settings to the extent that the individual needs of the student are met?

    (A) Zero reject
    (B) Due process
    (C) Individualized education
    (D) Least-restrictive environment

53. A 14 year old boy with mild autism would be LEAST likely to have which of the following components in his curriculum?

    (A) Functional academics on how to read bus schedules
    (B) Social-skills training in how to join a conversation
    (C) Reading instruction in a second-grade text
    (D) Career interest development

54. Natalie has occasional outbursts or temper tantrums during class. She tends to be disruptive because her outbursts often last for long periods of time. Her teacher wants to intervene but knows that it is important to do baseline assessment. The most useful type of assessment for this behavior would come from

    (A) interval recording
    (B) event recording
    (C) time sampling
    (D) duration recording

55. All of the following are the components of the AAMR definition of mental retardation EXCEPT

   (A) significantly subaverage intellectual performance
   (B) deficits in two or more areas of adaptive behavior
   (C) primarily genetic causation
   (D) manifestation during developmental period

56. Some students with disabilities have a tendency to give up because they think that they will fail no matter how hard they try. This phenomenon is known as

   (A) conduct disorder
   (B) learned helplessness
   (C) social maladjustment
   (D) metacognition

57. Which of the following activities would be LEAST likely to foster parent-teacher cooperation?

   (A) Inviting parents to participate in the classroom
   (B) Frequent communication
   (C) Listening to parents
   (D) Inviting all the student's teachers to the IEP meeting

58. An organization that was founded in 1922 to advocate for all children with disabilities was

   (A) Association for Retarded Citizens (ARC)
   (B) Council for Exceptional Children (CEC)
   (C) Learning Disabilities Association (LDA)
   (D) Children and Adults with Attention-Deficit/Hyperactivity Disorder (CHADD)

59. The approach that categorizes exceptionality as the statistical degree to which an individual deviates from the average in terms of cognitive, social-emotional, and physical abilities is called

   (A) sociological
   (B) cultural
   (C) developmental
   (D) individual

60. Andrea is a student with a mild conductive hearing loss. She is likely to make use of

   (A) a cochlear implant
   (B) ASL as her primary language
   (C) a hearing aid
   (D) a hearing guide dog

Chapter 6

Right Answers and Explanations for
the *Special Education: Core Knowledge*
Practice Questions

▶   ▶   ▶   ▶   ▶   ▶   ▶   ▶   ▶   ▶   ▶   ▶

Right Answers and Explanations for the Practice Questions

Question Number	Correct Answer	Content Category
1	C	Delivery of Services to Students with Disabilities
2	B	Delivery of Services to Students with Disabilities or Understanding Exceptionalities
3	A	Legal and Societal Issues
4	D	Legal and Societal Issues
5	B	Delivery of Services to Students with Disabilities
6	D	Delivery of Services to Students with Disabilities
7	D	Delivery of Services to Students with Disabilities or Understanding Exceptionalities
8	A	Understanding Exceptionalities
9	B	Delivery of Services to Students with Disabilities
10	C	Legal and Societal Issues
11	A	Understanding Exceptionalities
12	B	Legal and Societal Issues
13	C	Legal and Societal Issues
14	A	Delivery of Services to Students with Disabilities
15	B	Understanding Exceptionalities
16	A	Delivery of Services to Students with Disabilities
17	B	Delivery of Services to Students with Disabilities
18	D	Delivery of Services to Students with Disabilities
19	A	Delivery of Services to Students with Disabilities
20	B	Delivery of Services to Students with Disabilities
21	B	Delivery of Services to Students with Disabilities
22	C	Delivery of Services to Students with Disabilities
23	D	Delivery of Services to Students with Disabilities
24	A	Delivery of Services to Students with Disabilities
25	C	Understanding Exceptionalities
26	D	Understanding Exceptionalities
27	A	Understanding Exceptionalities
28	A	Delivery of Services to Students with Disabilities
29	D	Legal and Societal Issues
30	A	Delivery of Services to Students with Disabilities

Question Number	Correct Answer	Content Category
31	B	Delivery of Services to Students with Disabilities
32	D	Understanding Exceptionalities
33	A	Delivery of Services to Students with Disabilities
34	C	Understanding Exceptionalities
35	D	Understanding Exceptionalities or Delivery of Services to Students with Disabilities
36	C	Delivery of Services to Students with Disabilities
37	B	Delivery of Services to Students with Disabilities
38	B	Understanding Exceptionalities
39	D	Understanding Exceptionalities
40	A	Delivery of Services to Students with Disabilities
41	B	Delivery of Services to Students with Disabilities
42	C	Delivery of Services to Students with Disabilities
43	B	Legal and Societal Issues
44	C	Delivery of Services to Students with Disabilities
45	D	Delivery of Services to Students with Disabilities
46	B	Understanding Exceptionalities
47	A	Delivery of Services to Students with Disabilities
48	C	Delivery of Services to Students with Disabilities
49	B	Legal and Societal Issues
50	D	Legal and Societal Issues
51	A	Delivery of Services to Students with Disabilities
52	D	Legal and Societal Issues
53	C	Delivery of Services to Students with Disabilities
54	D	Delivery of Services to Students with Disabilities
55	C	Understanding Exceptionalities
56	B	Understanding Exceptionalities
57	D	Delivery of Services to Students with Disabilities
58	B	Legal and Societal Issues
59	C	Understanding Exceptionalities
60	C	Understanding Exceptionalities

Explanations of Right Answers

1. This question asks you to choose the most relevant information for designing individual instruction. Although scores from standardized tests (A), the category of the disability (B), and the amount of time spent in the resource room (D) may provide a degree of pertinent information about the student's overall functioning, none is directly connected to the curriculum and instruction the student currently receives. On the other hand, curriculum-based assessment tells the teacher how the student is performing on the current curriculum under current teaching conditions and is the most relevant for making decisions about curriculum and instruction. The correct answer, therefore, is (C).

2. This question tests your knowledge of characteristics and identification of disability categories. You should be able to rule out (A) because this student has average intelligence. Similarly, the profile is inconsistent with autistic behavior (D). Although it is possible that the student does have attention-deficit disorder (C), none of the information in the stem is used for diagnosing ADD. On the other hand, a discrepancy between ability and achievement is one of the primary characteristics in the identification of a specific learning disability. The correct answer, therefore, is (B).

3. This question tests your knowledge of the components of an IEP. Objectives in an IEP are ordinarily for a single year, which rules out (B). IEP's are plans, not guarantees, making (C) incorrect. Neither do IEP's contain budgets (D). On the other hand, the IEP is the document that provides for the least restrictive environment. A focus on inclusion in IDEA '97 begins with the assumption that the general classroom is usually the least restrictive environment; any other placement must be justified accordingly. The correct answer, therefore, is (A).

4. This question tests your understanding of inclusive approaches to education. Research has identified collaboration (A), diversity (B), and cooperative learning (C) as factors; these all seem reasonably connected with the effective inclusion of special education students in the general classroom. Inclusive education creates diverse, heterogeneous classrooms; it effectively rejects placing students together solely on the basis of disability category (D). The correct answer, therefore, is (D).

5. This question tests your understanding of transition planning. Jeff is pursuing activities that point him toward employment and independence. These activities do not indicate a need for increased support in adulthood [(C) and (D)]. Attending college (A) does not seem particularly relevant to these activities. Jeff may be pursuing a specific goal of becoming an electrician, or he may be getting general job experience. We can safely conclude that he is looking for skilled or semiskilled employment. The correct answer, therefore, is (B).

6. This question tests your knowledge of adaptive technology for persons who are blind. You can answer this question by a process of elimination. The terms in (A), (B), and (C) indicate an association with movement. Additionally, you should recognize that an Optacon scanner converts written text into tactile reproductions. Consequently, the Optacon scanner would not be used in mobility training. The correct answer, therefore, is (D).

7. This question tests both your knowledge of the AAMR definition of mental retardation and your understanding of psychoeducational measures. Mental retardation involves both subaverage intellectual functioning and limitations in two or more adaptive skills areas. Only one answer, (D), includes a measure to assess intelligence (Stanford-Binet) and a measure to assess adaptive behavior (Scales of Independent Behavior). The correct answer, therefore, is (D).

8. This question tests your familiarity with various physical disabilities. The question gives you two significant pieces of information, each of which independently provides the answer. In addition, of the choices, the term "spina" seems logically related to "spinal." While you should not rely on possible embedded answers, the connection should reinforce your selection of spina bifida. The correct answer, therefore, is (A).

9. This question asks you to make a general connection between curriculum and characteristics. Although one or two components of the curriculum would possibly be appropriate for students with various types of disabilities, augmentative communication is not a common support for students with learning disabilities (A), emotional disorders (C), or ADD/ADHD (D). The particular combination of functional behaviors utilizing extensive parent support would apply to students with more involved disabilities. The correct answer, therefore, is (B).

10. This question addresses precedents that have influenced the basic constructs of special education legislation. Concerns about evaluation and instruction of Hispanic American students (*Diana* v. *State Board of Education*), African American students (*Larry P.* v. *Riles*), and Asian American students (*Lau* v. *Nichols*) helped to craft the tenet of nondiscriminatory assessment of students from diverse cultural backgrounds. The correct answer, therefore, is (C).

11. This question tests your understanding of a critical conceptual component of learning disabilities. The conceptual framework is that students with learning disabilities are intelligent, but they have specific learning problems that interfere with achievement in particular subject areas. Although controversy exists about the use of a discrepancy approach in the identification of learning disabilities, most examiners compare scores on standardized ability or intelligence tests with scores on standardized tests of achievement. CBA may actually offer more authentic representation of student work, but it is not used as a definitive component of the discrepancy approach. If the scores on standardized ability tests are higher than scores

on standardized achievement tests (and other causes can be ruled out), the student may be identified as learning disabled. The correct answer, therefore, is (A).

12. This question requires that you understand that IDEA '97 did not alter the fundamental principles of (A) and (C). IDEA '97 did mandate transition planning by age 14, (D). Although IDEA '97 may provide services to students through 21 years of age, those services are almost always part of the K-12 public school system. IDEA '97 does not require IEP's for college students with disabilities. The correct answer, therefore, is (B).

13. This question tests whether you can apply the *Rowley* case to a more general principle. In *Rowley*, a student who was deaf was denied an interpreter because she was achieving satisfactorily without one. This ruling demonstrated that "appropriate education" does not mean the best education [(A) and (B)]. It also showed that deaf students do not automatically get interpreters (D). Rather, it made clear that as long as students with special needs are doing as well as their peers, they are receiving an appropriate education. The correct answer, therefore, is (C).

14. This question explores some of the differences between mainstreaming and inclusion. In the mainstreaming model, students with disabilities often receive services outside of the general education classroom, frequently in the resource room. Students with disabilities attend the general education classroom only when they are able to function independently

in that setting. An inclusive approach begins with the assumption that all students have the right to be educated in the general education classroom. In this model, the special education teacher works with the general education teacher in the general education classroom. The special education teacher is able to provide services to students without removing them from the general education classroom. The correct answer, therefore, is (A).

15. This question focuses on the term "functional." Deafness can be defined in terms of hearing loss (decibel threshold), but (D) refers to frequencies, not loudness. Functional deafness is not about hearing sounds per se, (A). It certainly is not about problems with lipreading, (C); many deaf persons can lip-read well. However, when a hearing loss interferes with understanding and using spoken language, it becomes a functional issue that warrants special education services. The correct answer, therefore, is (B).

16. This question asks you to be aware of a significant area of instruction for students with disabilities. Social skills instruction often serves as the basis for educational success in the inclusive classroom. Teaching social skills requires the same skills as those used in all areas of education. Social skills training does not receive as much attention in general education, but recognition of its importance to the success of inclusive education is growing. The correct answer, therefore, is (A).

17. This question looks at the most common approach to classroom management, a behavior-oriented program. According to a behavioral explanation, reinforcement, (A), including negative reinforcement, (C), only maintains or increases the inappropriate behavior. (D) could be incorporated at some point, but a behavioral approach involves an active, measurable plan. (B) allows the teacher to increase an appropriate behavior that excludes the inappropriate one. The correct answer, therefore, is (B).

18. This question highlights a fundamental shift in philosophy and responsibility in a full-inclusion program. In full inclusion, the student spends the entire day in the general education classroom, which rules out (A) and (B). However, the student still receives necessary additional support in the general education classroom, ruling out (C). An important change in inclusive programs is that the special education teacher no longer is the sole teacher with primary responsibility for the student with special needs. Instead, the general education teacher assumes much of the responsibility for the student's education. The correct answer, therefore, is (D).

19. This question asks you to think about the type of instruction Shania receives in the context of her grade level. Direct instruction in decoding skills is not typical instruction in the tenth grade; it is more typical in elementary settings. This method does not provide compensations in order to access the normal tenth-grade curriculum, (B). It is not holistic, (C), nor does it focus on different learning modalities, (D),

such as auditory or visual. It does attempt to remediate by teaching fundamental skills. The correct answer, therefore, is (A).

20. This question tests your familiarity with the Woodcock-Johnson Psychoeducational Battery, Revised (WJ), as well as your understanding of typical testing in the identification of learning disabilities. The entire battery consists of both cognitive and achievement sections. It can provide a discrepancy score between ability and achievement, which is typically a major component of the diagnosis of learning disabilities. The correct answer, therefore, is (B). (Note that some districts do not accept the WJ as a sufficient measure of ability, but require a WISC, Kauffman, or Stanford-Binet.)

21. This question tests your knowledge of different kinds of individual plans as well as your recognition of commonly used acronyms. An IEP, (A), is an educational plan for use with students who are in school. An ITP, (C), is a transition plan, usually beginning with students who are 14. An ISP, (D), is a service plan for adults who have exited the school system. In working with infants and toddlers, it is critical to involve the whole family, as that is where the child spends the most time. The IFSP is an individualized family service plan, the most appropriate approach for working with young children. The correct answer, therefore, is (B).

22. This question asks you to distinguish teacher-directed from student-centered instructional approaches. Cooperative learning, (A), cross-age tutoring, (B), and study-skills groups, (D),

all rely on students' taking active roles and interacting with each other. Direct instruction is an approach in which the teacher uses precisely sequenced lessons that involve only student-teacher interactions. The correct answer, therefore, is (C).

23. This question provides several answers that may be true in some circumstances but only one answer that is true in all cases. That is, (A), (B), and (C) all can be used to support and improve communication, but each represents a fairly specific means or approach. On the other hand, augmentative communication is the more general approach that encompasses many different methods to build or augment communication. The correct answer, therefore, is (D).

24. This question emphasizes that assistive technology is not always "hi-tech." Use of a tape recorder and calculator does allow the student to access grade-level material, ruling out (C). While these devices do help the student become more independent, they are not a part of a self-management plan, (D), nor are they computer-related, (B). These devices are relatively simple but effective examples of assistive technology. The correct answer, therefore, is (A).

25. This question touches on a major concern in the field of communication disorders. Articulation disorders are by far the most prevalent of all communication disorders. However, many young children make articulation errors as a normal part of speech development. Some professionals believe that articulation disorders should be treated only in students 10 or older, which would undoubtedly reduce the prevalence. Nevertheless, at the present time, many young children receive services for articulation disorders. The correct answer, therefore, is (C).

26. This question explores an underlying theme in dealing with persons with severe and multiple disabilities. Many of these individuals require specialized and intensive instruction in order to acquire and use basic skills because they have diminished learning and memory capabilities. Although individuals may have multiple disabilities that do not include mental retardation, mental retardation is relatively pervasive in this population. The correct answer, therefore, is (D).

27. This question is a relatively straightforward knowledge item, testing your awareness that the vast majority of students with mental retardation have mild mental retardation. The implications of this fact are significant. Most students with mental retardation do not go to special schools; special education teachers may need to help prepare general education teachers to work with these students in the general education classroom. Many people have stereotypes of Down syndrome as typical of mental retardation. In reality, most students with mental retardation are not that different from other students. The correct answer, therefore, is (A).

28. This question highlights an approach that many teachers use for specific instructional purposes and planning. By focusing on the student's work in class and on the curriculum, the teacher is assessing the student in the context of the current instruction (A). If the student is not achieving objectives, the teacher can use curriculum-based assessment as a basis for modifying or adapting instruction. The correct answer, therefore, is (A).

29. This question requires a fairly specific understanding of IDEA '97. Although students with ADD/ADHD may access services under the IDEA category of Other Health Impairments or through "504 plans," Congress has yet to include it as a specific disability category. (A), (B), and (C) are all provisions in IDEA '97. The correct answer, therefore, is (D).

30. This question asks you to distinguish approaches to grouping students with disabilities. In a cross-categorical approach, (B), students with different disability categories but similar instructional needs are placed together. A noncategorical approach, (C), avoids specific labeling altogether. Placing students with the same disabilities together may not be consistent with current interpretations of the least restrictive environment, (D), but it does define the categorical approach to special education. The correct answer, therefore, is (A).

31. This question tests your understanding of a behavioral approach to changing behavior. Many teachers understand the use of consequences, both positive and negative, on behavior, (A). However, this did not work for the teacher. Rather than spending more time building what are oftentimes elaborate reward systems, the teacher discovered that taking away the cause of the problem (i.e., their proximity to each other) changed the behavior, (B). The teacher did not focus on ignoring the behavior, (C), or on using a reinforcing activity, (D). The correct answer, therefore, is (B).

32. This question focuses on the broadening of the definition of mental retardation. IQ tests are far from perfect and may not predict overall or adaptive functioning. Consequently, the AAMR includes deficits in adaptive skills as a critical component. (A) applies to students with learning disabilities. (B) and (C) are much rarer in people with mental retardation than generally assumed. The correct answer, therefore, is (D).

33. This question tests your knowledge of approaches to classroom management. Functional assessment (B) identifies antecedents, consequences, and settings and is usually conducted by the teacher. Reality therapy, (C), involves an interview of the student by the teacher. An ecological assessment, (D), examines the individual's interaction with the environment. Contingency-based self-management makes the student responsible for monitoring behavior and may be particularly effective for students with ADHD. The correct answer, therefore, is (A).

34. This question centers on your understanding of the terms *receptive* and *language disorder*. Both (A) and (B) refer to possible expressive, not receptive, language disorders. While (D) could result in some kind of language problem, the most logical conclusion is that the behavior is due to a hearing problem rather than difficulty with language processing per se. However, a student who is looking to see what other students are doing may be having difficulty processing spoken language. The correct answer, therefore, is (C).

35. This question examines different theoretical explanations of behavior disorders. A phenomenological approach would focus on self-concept, (A). Behaviorists posit that all behavior is learned, (B). Neurological abnormalities would fit best with the biological perspective, (C). A psychoanalytic approach would take into account internal motivations and feelings, which are shaped by early childhood experiences. The correct answer, therefore, is (D).

36. This question essentially gives you a definition of direct instruction. Direct instruction is teacher-centered, which rules out (D). It does not focus exclusively on executive functioning, (A). It does not use assessment to diagnose specific processing problems, an approach associated with diagnostic-prescriptive teaching (B). The correct answer, therefore, is (C).

37. This question explores the type of role that an occupational therapist plays. Occupational therapy is not career counseling. Although it is concerned with instruction related to potential work activities, therapists also help students develop basic habilitative and independence skills. (A), (C), and (D) do not address these types of skills. (B) does. The correct answer, therefore, is (B).

38. This question looks at the relation between ADD/ADHD and learning disabilities. While there is not universal agreement on an exact number, most professionals estimate that about two-thirds of children with attention-deficit disorder or attention-deficit/hyperactivity disorder also have some kind of learning disability. Children with ADD/ADHD often have some type of behavior difficulty, but most do not exhibit specific conduct disorders, (A). Almost all children identified with ADD or ADHD are of normal intelligence, which rules out (C). They do not have unusual tics or twitches, (D). The correct answer, therefore, is (B).

39. This question underscores the fact that if you are a special education teacher, it is highly likely that you will teach at least some students with learning disabilities. Students with learning disabilities make up the largest single category in special education. According to the 18th Report to Congress of IDEA (1996), of the 4,915,168 students between 6 and 21 receiving special education services, 2,513,977, or slightly more than 50 percent, were classified as having learning disabilities. The correct answer, therefore, is (D).

40. This question suggests that before educators rush to label a student to grant eligibility for special education services, they should examine whether the student can function in the general education setting with minor modifications. That is, before deciding that there is a problem, educators should do informal observations and screening. (B) and (D) represent decisions based on insufficient information at this moment. It is to be hoped that principals would not generally adopt the practice of (C). The correct answer, therefore, is (A).

41. This question illustrates a dilemma faced by many students with mild hearing loss. These students often function quite well in face-to-face situations where they make use of many communication cues. As a result, teachers and others may forget that the hearing loss is significant. Turning away from a student with a mild hearing loss may break down communication significantly. Chelsea does not need the teacher to shout in her ear, (A), which could also be humiliating. As a student with a mild hearing loss, she is unlikely to use sign language as a primary means of communication, (C). Having another student write down assignments, (D), takes away Chelsea's responsibility and might lead to learned helplessness. Making sure Chelsea has communication cues she can use seems most sensible. The correct answer, therefore, is (B).

42. This question assesses your understanding of using informal reading inventories (IRI's). Because Nicky's instructional level is within the third grade, fifth-grade reading material is not appropriate, (A). Although he might be able to

read up to the 4.2 level, fourth-grade material is also likely to frustrate him, (B). He is able to read, however, and excusing him from reading is inappropriate, (D). Finding instructional material at his independent/instructional level is the best way to use the reading skill that he does have. The correct answer, therefore, is (C).

43. This question poses a situation in which a student takes a test that is not in his native language. The principle of nondiscriminatory assessment, (B), exists to ensure that scores are valid indicators of a student's ability. An IQ test that is not administered in the student's native language is not necessarily measuring intelligence; the score may reflect difficulty with the English language. Principles in (A), (C), and (D) are not concerned with this specific issue of testing in the student's native language. The correct answer, therefore, is (B).

44. This question focuses on teaching functional skills to older students with disabilities. (A) and (D) refer to basic writing skills, but they are not tied to a specific, practical application. (B) is a functional skill but is unlikely to be relevant for the majority of students with mild mental retardation. On the other hand, most of these students will be entering the workforce. Learning how to fill out an application is a critical first step. The correct answer, therefore, is (C).

45. This question tests your understanding of negative reinforcement. Negative reinforcement is designed to maintain or increase a behavior by removing an aversive

stimulus when the target behavior occurs. It is not designed to decrease or extinguish behaviors. (A), (B), and (C) all involve negative consequences, but negative consequences are quite different from negative reinforcement. The correct answer, therefore, is (D).

46. This question asks you to differentiate theories that are applied to emotional and behavioral disorders. Both humanistic, (C), and psychoanalytic, (D), perspectives focus on the individual's feelings and motivations rather than on interactions with the environment. Behavioral perspectives, (A), acknowledge the impact of the environment but concentrate on the learning of new, appropriate behavior. The ecological model, with some behavioral underpinnings, examines interactions of the student and the environment. The correct answer, therefore, is (B).

47. This question highlights a behavioral technique for working with groups of students. In many ways, almost all teachers use contingencies: rewards are contingent upon demonstrating desired behaviors, or goals. Contingencies can be applied to group behavior as well as individual. Operant conditioning, (B), while it may incorporate contingencies, is too broad a term. Response cost, (C), focuses more on withholding or removing privileges as a consequence for inappropriate behavior. Cognitive behavior modification, (D), is a technique for acquiring specific educational skills, usually used in one-to-one teaching. The correct answer, therefore, is (A).

48. This question explores the purpose for assessing adaptive behavior. Students who are gifted and talented, (A), are identified most often through teacher recommendation and possibly IQ testing. Testing for learning disabilities, (B), usually involves aptitude and achievement measures. Fragile X syndrome, (D), is identified through genetic testing. The diagnosis of mental retardation depends not only on significantly subaverage intellectual functioning but also on concurrent deficits in adaptive behavior, as measured on instruments such as the Vineland. The correct answer, therefore, is (C).

49. This question emphasizes that transition planning encompasses more than simply the transition from school to work. IDEA '97 defines transition planning as a coordinated set of activities leading to outcomes in post-school activities: postsecondary education, vocational training, integrated employment, continuing and adult education, adult services, independent living, or community participation. The IEP, (A), may contain transition planning, but it is a much broader document. The IFSP, (C), generally is used with families of infants and toddlers. The REI, (D), was Madeline Will's initiative that spurred practices of inclusion. The correct answer, therefore, is (B).

50. This question tackles an often thorny issue in education. Suspending a student because of a disability is a form of discrimination. It is not an issue of nondiscriminatory assessment, (B). Parents are not playing a role in this decision, (C), and no mention is made of timelines or other concerns pertinent to due process, (A). Zero reject, (D), the principle that every student is entitled to a free and appropriate education (F.A.P.E.) and that no student can be rejected or denied an education because of a disability, does support the administration's rationale and decision. The correct answer, therefore, is (D).

51. This question asks you to identify the whole-language approach to reading instruction. A key in this question is the differentiation of this approach from ones that break down reading into a collection of separate skills. (B), (C), and (D) all approach reading by strengthening component skills of reading. In contrast, whole-language instruction emphasizes a holistic approach, in which all instruction focuses on reading for meaning. The correct answer, therefore, is (A).

52. This question examines the current construct of the least restrictive environment. Under PL 94-142, the least restrictive environment was the setting closest to the mainstream that met student needs. By the time of IDEA '97, the idea had evolved that all students have the right to be educated in, not near, the general education setting. Connected with the inclusion philosophy, this current notion means that support, services, and adjustments are provided within the general education classroom. The correct answer, therefore, is (D).

53. This question asks you to be aware of age-appropriate activities. For a 14-year-old student, (A), (B), and (D) all address issues that are relevant to a teenager. Reading from a second-grade text, even though his reading ability may be poor, is not age appropriate for Benjamin. Adapting material or using high-interest low-vocabulary reading texts would be more sensible. The correct answer, therefore, is (C).

54. This question tests your knowledge of different observational recording techniques. Natalie's tantrums are disruptive because of the length or duration of time involved, not so much because of how often they occur. (A), (B), and (C) are all different ways of assessing the frequency of a behavior, which is not the teacher's focus. Duration recording, (D), provides the amount of time a student engages in a behavior. By knowing duration, the teacher can set reasonable goals so that Natalie can reduce the length of the disruptive behavior until it is extinguished or at least not disruptive. The correct answer, therefore, is (D).

55. This question tests your knowledge of both the definition of mental retardation and a myth of mental retardation. The AAMR definition refers to intellect, (A), adaptive behavior, (B), and developmental period, (D), in conceptualizing mental retardation. Contrary to popular belief, genetic factors are not the primary known cause; the cause of mental retardation in most individuals is cultural-familial. The correct answer, therefore, is (C).

56. This question addresses a characteristic shared by a number of students with disabilities. This behavior of giving up, combined with the deficits associated with disabilities, presents a significant challenge to special education teachers. Most educators believe this behavior is learned, a learned helplessness, (B). (A) and (C) are problematic behaviors but not specifically connected with giving up. (D) refers to executive functioning or self-monitoring. The correct answer, therefore, is (B).

57. This question examines parent-teacher relationships. (A), (B), and (C) all suggest ways to bring parents into the educational process. The teacher is not setting the agenda but rather is empowering the parents. Inviting all the student's teachers to the IEP meeting would likely have the opposite effect. Being outnumbered may put parents on the defensive. The correct answer, therefore, is (D).

58. This question tests your familiarity with advocacy and professional organizations for individuals with learning disabilities. If you know the founding dates of all the different organizations (ARC, 1950; CEC, 1922; LDA, 1964; CHADD, 1987), you will answer the question correctly. You may also determine the correct answer by focusing on "all children with disabilities," which effectively rules out (A), (C), and (D). The correct answer, therefore, is (B).

59. This question looks at how we decide what is normal and what is not. A sociological approach, (A), would focus on how individuals deviate from social standards. A cultural approach, (B), would examine the dominant cultural values and how they may conflict with other cultural values. Exceptionality may also be self-defined, (D). The developmental approach compares an individual's growth pattern to a group average, thereby providing developmental norms and milestones. The correct answer, therefore, is (C).

60. This question asks that you understand some of the implications of a mild conductive hearing loss. A conductive loss, associated with mechanical transmission of sound in the middle ear, tends to respond to a hearing aid. With a mild loss, the prognosis is even better. (A) may be appropriate for some individuals with a sensorineural (rather than conductive) hearing loss. (B) and (D) are generally appropriate to persons with moderate to severe hearing loss. The correct answer, therefore, is (C).

Chapter 7
Are You Ready? Last-Minute Tips

► ► ► ► ► ► ► ► ► ► ►

Checklist

❏ Do you know the testing requirements for your teaching field in the state(s) where you plan to teach?

❏ Have you followed all of the test registration procedures?

❏ Do you know the topics that will be covered in each test you plan to take?

❏ Have you reviewed any textbooks, class notes, and course readings that relate to the topics covered?

❏ Do you know how long the test will take and the number of questions it contains? Have you considered how you will pace your work?

❏ Are you familiar with the test directions and the types of questions for your test?

❏ Are you familiar with the recommended test-taking strategies and tips?

❏ Have you practiced by working through the practice test questions at a pace similar to that of an actual test?

❏ If constructed-response questions are part of your test, do you understand the scoring criteria for these items?

❏ If you are repeating a Praxis Series™ Assessment, have you analyzed your previous score report to determine areas where additional study and test preparation could be useful?

The Day of the Test

You should have ended your review a day or two before the actual test date. And many clichés you may have heard about the day of the test are true. You should

- Be well rested

- Take photo identification with you

- Take a supply of well-sharpened #2 pencils (at least three)

- Eat before you take the test

- Be prepared to stand in line to check in or to wait while other test takers are being checked in

You can't control the testing situation, but you can control yourself. Stay calm. The supervisors are well trained and make every effort to provide uniform testing conditions, but don't let it bother you if the test doesn't start exactly on time. You will have the necessary amount of time once it does start.

You can think of preparing for this test as training for an athletic event. Once you've trained, and prepared, and rested, give it everything you've got. Good luck.

Appendix A
Study Plan Sheet

▶ ▶ ▶ ▶ ▶ ▶ ▶ ▶ ▶ ▶ ▶ ▶

Study Plan Sheet

See chapter 1 for suggestions on using this Study Plan Sheet.

STUDY PLAN						
Content covered on test	How well do I know the content?	What material do I have for studying this content?	What material do I need for studying this content?	Where could I find the materials I need?	Dates planned for study of content	Dates completed

Appendix B
For More Information

Educational Testing Service offers additional information to assist you in preparing for The Praxis Series™ Assessments. The *Registration Bulletin* is available without charge (see below to order). You can also obtain more information, and review *Tests at a Glance* by visiting our Web site: www.ets.org/praxis.

General Inquiries

Phone: 800-772-9476 or 609-771-7395 (Monday-Friday, 8:00 A.M. to 7:45 P.M., Eastern time)
Fax: 609-771-7906

Extended Time

If you have a learning disability or if English is not your primary language, you can apply to be given more time to take your test. The *Registration Bulletin* tells you how you can qualify for extended time.

Disability Services

Phone: 866-387-8602 or 609-771-7780
Fax: 609-771-7906
TTY (for deaf or hard-of-hearing callers): 609-771-7714

Mailing Address

ETS—The Praxis Series
P.O. Box 6051
Princeton, NJ 08541-6051

Overnight Delivery Address

ETS—The Praxis Series
Distribution Center
225 Phillips Blvd.
Ewing, NJ 08628

NOTES

NOTES

NOTES

NOTES